The A - Z Guide for Porcelain Painters

'What is it and why did I buy it?'

Di Teasdale

The A - Z Guide for Porcelain Painters

Tricia Bradford

Kangaroo Press

Acknowledgements

It would not have been possible to compile this book without the help of many people, some well known to me and others who will remain forever unknown. Much of the information came from artists and students who, like myself, had read or heard some item of interest and filed it away in the labyrinth of their minds; their source of information was almost certainly not the original one and it is therefore not possible to acknowledge these people by name. We can only thank them.

I can and do thank the many commercial people who gave their time and support in supplying me with information about their products. Good friends like Doug Lang of Alexanders, Fay Good, Celia Larsen and Sandra Brown, who not only allowed me to use the material from her book but gave me a copy as well! And Josephine Robinson, of Gilberton Gallery, who generously keeps me supplied with her wonderful brushes, the only ones I will use.

There were also the people whom I do not know well who gave their valuable time to assist. Peter Pritchard of Degussa, when I said I was ignorant about gold, kindly sent me 3 kilograms of information! Thanks to Tetlow's we have a comprehensive set of instructions for firing. Porcelain Art Importers Pty Ltd were kind enough to let us know about Floral products. And of course many many others whose products you will read about and now know how the manufacturer suggests they be used. I cannot mention them all by name as I would like to, but I thank them and suggest that we support them so that they may continue to support us.

Lastly, but certainly not least, two dear friends who took upon themselves the onerous task of proof reading and correcting both my grammar and my spelling! My heartfelt thanks to Yvonne Hammond and Dr David Mackenzie who also acted as my technical adviser.

Reprinted 1991
First published in 1989 by Kangaroo Press Pty Ltd
3 Whitehall Road (P.O. Box 75) Kenthurst 2156
Typeset by Midland Typesetters Pty Ltd
Printed in Hong Kong by Colorcraft Ltd

ISBN 0 86417 266 4

Contents

Foreword

'Honour' and 'privilege' are hackneyed words these days, but after long consideration I have decided that they were still the most appropriate words to describe my feelings upon being asked to write the foreword to Tricia Bradford's fifth book.

All china decorators have benefited from Trish's previous publications; her current book will be no exception. It is a well known fact that we 'onglaze decorators' have a greater variety of mediums available for our use than most artists. This dictionary expands our choice beyond imagination.

Trish has recognised the need for a glossary of terms so that all aspiring artists and active painters can communicate using universal terms. Teacher and pupil alike will find it invaluable.

Any delusions of competence I may have had were shattered by my initial scanning of this book. One of the first words I encountered was 'arcanist'—complete ignorance on my part, but of complete relevance to our art! After further reading I decided that a new term should be entered in the 'P' section: P for Pure Pleasure. This dictionary is a gem indeed. The research required to compile such a comprehensive glossary of terms and products used in onglaze art must be enormous.

For many years now, all onglaze artists have owed Tricia Bradford a debt for the pleasure and information that her books have given us; for faces and characters given to artists who were previously only known by name and for bringing together these artists from different States. How gratifying it is to visit libraries around Australia and find her books on the shelves with other art publications.

You will find that this new book will be in constant use—a 'teacher in residence' on your shelf or, better still, in your workbox.

Thanks again, Trish, for a big job well done, as usual.

Beverley Ambridge

Introduction

'A survival manual for aspiring artists.'

This book is a combination of facts, figures, definitions and descriptions and my reason for writing it is that I have a lot of basic knowledge about the art of painting on porcelain, however whenever I wanted to reinforce or verify that knowledge I could never remember where I had read or heard about it or else I could not find the particular article or book in my chaotic library. Obviously there was a need for organisation in my life and library and rather than make a catalogue, which I had tried at one stage but soon became tired of, I decided to collect all this information and keep it in a book and keep the book in my box of tricks! Maybe some of you have similar problems!

Collecting information was surprisingly interesting. It involved going through and skim reading every book, article and magazine I had and could borrow, and my Father once said that I was the sort of person who should never clean out the attic because I read everything, even the labels on jam tins. Obviously, it would be impossible to differentiate between what I knew beforehand and what I gleaned from others, and to determine where information originated; there is so much that is said and written, passed on and reiterated that it becomes a melange of fact, fantasy, rumour and myth, some of which works for some people and not for others.

Which brings me to the variables! And the most important variable is the human factor. When following a recipe for cooking, if one does not adhere strictly to the instructions the flavour is a little different, and you may or may not like the result. In porcelain art if you do not follow the instructions the same thing happens, only here the matter is complicated by other variables such as amount of paint or paste, thickness applied, drying time, kiln, time/temperature curve, position in kiln and so on. They are endless, these variables; even the china on which we paint gives different results and the products we use may have similar names but be from different manufacturers and their chemical content is very likely entirely different. Two artists, sitting side by side, using exactly the same materials, painting the same subject, will produce two dissimilar results.

Therefore, when you read this book and any other reference material, please keep in mind the factors which affect your work and make allowances.

Many of the terms used refer specifically to porcelain and the art of painting on it. Obviously, it would not have been practical to fill the book with terminology and give irrelevant definitions or meanings which refer to other activities. We have quite enough weight to carry around with us as it is!

The other limitations in this book are that I have only given brief and basic instructions for many of the techniques used. If you require further information, you will undoubtedly find it in one of the many books written on the subject. However, using the instructions included here and a little experimentation, you should be able to produce the effects you are looking for; your work will be all the more individual if you develop your own methods of application.

'Learn all you can from the mistakes of others. You will not live long enough to make them all yourself.'

Tricia Bradford

The A - Z Guide for Porcelain Painters

Abbozo   Oil painting term adapted to porcelain. First underpainting, frequently painted in monochrome.

Abstract   Concerned with pure form and pattern. Adaptation from the visible world in which shape, line and colour are given more emphasis than is evident in the subject being painted. It is only occasionally possible to identify the original model. There are many ways of approaching an abstract drawing as it depends on how the individual artist sees an object, however, simplification of a whole or part of the object is one easy way. This may then be extended to fit into the space you wish to fill.

Abstract expressionism   The expression of emotion in art as opposed to reality.

Accent   Strength with line or colour to emphasise detail and to attract attention.

Achromatic colours   Black, white and grey are termed achromatic colours as opposed to chromatic colours.

Acid etch powder   *To etch the porcelain.* Mask that part of the porcelain which is *not* to be etched with Cover Coat or masking lacquer. Mix a small amount of acid etch powder with medium to a milky consistency and paint it over the area to be etched. Pad gently with silk covered pad. Remove Cover Coat or lacquer and fire at 760°C.
Carey's product To use, draw or trace design and apply Cover Coat over parts of porcelain *not* to be etched. Mix a small amount of the powder with Seminar medium just thin enough to paint and brush it over the exposed porcelain. Pad with silk over cotton wool and remove Cover Coat. Fire to 760°C.

Acid etching   To remove glaze from a piece of porcelain with the aid of hydrofluoric acid. The area where the glaze is removed will be matt in contrast to the high gloss in untouched areas.

Caution: Etching with hydrofluoric acid. Sketch a design the size of the required etching and transfer it by tracing with the aid of graphite paper onto the porcelain. Using asphaltum paint the area *not to be etched*, completely covering the porcelain to protect it from the acid. Take care to see that the asphaltum is thick enough, and that there are no holes or brown areas. Cover all the porcelain not to be etched including the back or base of the piece. The asphaltum may have to be thinned from time to time to keep it flowing. Allow to dry a day or so and then place the object into an acid bath of 50% hydrofluoric acid for 1-2 minutes or until the etching is deep enough. Remove, and wash under running water to neutralise the acid. Wash with kerosene and then with hot soapy water to remove all traces of asphaltum and fire to further clean the porcelain. Please read more detailed instructions for etching than these if you wish to etch with acid. (*Porcelain Art in Australia Today*)

To etch with etching cream. Proceed as above until asphaltum has completely dried and then apply etching cream thickly over the areas to be etched. Leave for 12 to 24 hours, testing occasionally the depth of the etch. Clean as above. Although Etchall cream is a commercial preparation no longer available, similar preparations should be treated with *extreme caution* as burns will result from the cream just as from the solution. If acid comes into contact with your skin wash immediately in soda, soap and water to neutralise it. If severe, seek medical attention.

Acid, hydrofluoric   *Caution*: Very dangerous acid which should be used with extreme care to etch glass and remove colour from fired china. Always use plastic or rubber gloves, protective clothing and work in the open air or by an open window. If the acid comes in contact with the skin painful burns will result and the fumes can be harmful if inhaled. *See* Rustiban, Hydrofluoric acid, Etching.

Acid under base   Floral product. A texture paste applied with a sponge, brush or pen to the porcelain surface and fired at 780°-815°C to give an etched look without the use of acid. Gold or lustre may be applied over the matt area.

Acids   Silica, boron, antimony, tin, chromium, titanium and zircon are the most commonly used acids in the porcelain world. The acids combine with bases and neutrals and interact during the firing process to form a glaze.

Action painting   Broad sweeps of the brush to cover a large surface. Strong, forceful application of paint. (Difficult for the porcelain artist on our 'canvas' where space is limited and heavy applications of paint will chip off after firing.)

Aerial perspective   Distance implied by painting in pale and cool colours, eg blues, greys and mauves, and ill defined or blurred objects.

Aerograph   Spray gun for applying paint in a fine mist.

Afterimage   When the retina of the eye views a colour for any length of time it will eventually transmit an image of the complementary colour.

Agate burnisher   Agate set in a handle for burnishing or etching gold or metallic paint. The agate is rubbed on the gilded or painted surface to polish and bring it to a perfect shine.

Agate etching   Highlighting portion of a design painted in gold. Several coats of burnishing gold are applied to a piece of porcelain with each separate application being fired, burnished and rinsed thoroughly before the next is applied. Pen a design using powder paint mixed with pen oil to the consistency of ink, or with an ordinary HB pencil if you need guidelines. Fire and then highlight areas of the design with an agate etcher. This looks rather like a thick pencil with an amber coloured stone tip. Rubbing the tip on the gold will change and highlight the colour of the metal.

Airbrush   Equipment for applying paint in a fine mist. It consists of a 'brush' or small container of paint and fine spray gun and a container of compressed air, which is available in small cans or from a compressor. While smaller compressors do not have pressure gauges, large compressors do and, depending on the type of paint, the depth of colour and rate of delivery, the pressure should range from 15 to 40 lbs. Select a low rate and increase it until you are satisfied with the delivery of the paint. Paints may be mixed with alcohol which dries rapidly and allows several layers to be applied. Other solutions may be used and you may like to experiment until you find the one most suitable for you. All gritty particles must be removed from the solution, otherwise the minute grains will clog the nozzle of the airbrush. Strain the paint through layers of nylon stocking, and for particularly gritty paints mix with a mortar and pestle. Paints mixed with alcohol may be dehydrated by pouring off the solution and drying the wet paint on a tile; they are then returned to a phial and used as normal for conventional painting.

Airbrushing   Clean your porcelain well prior to using the airbrush as all grease and finger marks will show. Hold the airbrush approximately 30 cm (12″) from the article to be painted and depress the lever. Paint will spray in a fine mist from the nozzle. Move the airbrush in a sweeping motion so that the paint covers the surface to be painted. By turning the article or changing the angle of the airbrush, you have some control over the placement and direction of the paint. Allow time for the paint to dry between coats.

Alcohol   Colourless, volatile, inflammable fluid used among other things for cleaning porcelain blanks prior to painting. May be used occasionally to clean brushes thoroughly; however, continual cleaning with alcohol will destroy the natural oil in the hairs.

Alkali   In porcelain art, an alkali such as soda is used as a flux. Potash and lithia are also used. Soda will also intensify the colour. Baking soda can be used where you would normally use flux to adhere incising glass beads to lift the glaze, and to adhere sand, stones etc.

All'antica   Painting in an antique manner.

Alla prima   Italian term for a 'one fire painting' or painting completed in one session.

Analogous colour scheme   Colours adjacent on the colour wheel which blend well because of their basic shade. Usually no more than three or four are used at one time.

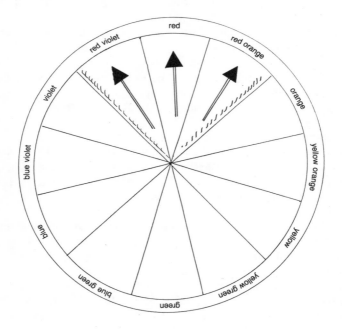

Angled strokes   For cross hatching. Turn the brush to a 45°angle and pull in that direction then in the opposite direction.

An-hua   Chinese term meaning hidden or secret decoration.

Anther   The foremost part of the stamen of a flower containing pollen and pollen sacs. *See* diagram on next page.

Anthropomorphic   To give human characteristics to inanimate objects and animal or plant life.

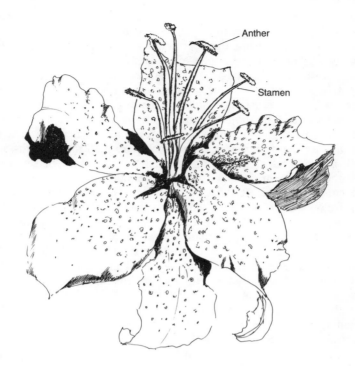

Anther

Stamen

Antique etch   Product which gives an appearance of erosion with age. Apply with an eye dropper or brush to cleaned greenware that will fire to 1005°C. *See* Carey's products.

Aqueous   To contain water or be soluble in water. Powder paint mixed with water soluble mediums and applied with similar vehicles.

Arabesque   Decoration composed of flowing lines and elaborate tracery.

Araldite   Two-part glue usually used for jewellery findings and bases of urns etc.
To dissolve. To unstick an object, place it in an oven which has been preheated to 350°F for 10 minutes for jewellery, longer for larger pieces; flick medallions out with pointed knife. If some paste jewellery or scrolling has popped off, colour some Araldite with the correct colour powder paint, allow to set until it holds its shape and repair your jewelling or scrolling as with enamel.

Arcanist   A person with the knowledge of porcelain making. The dictionary definition of 'arcane' is 'secret', and 'mysterious' which leads me to think of artisans locked away, unable to have contact with the rest of the world, so that they would not share their secrets.

Art fundamentals The basis of aesthetically pleasing artwork. Knowing the principles to abide by and developing an intuitive and artistic approach using these principles will increase your ability to paint well. The basic principles of art are:

Design, usually composed of a theme or subject, a mass, lines of direction, negative and positive space, a centre of interest, areas of additional or supporting interest and values of shading either in colour or greys. Think in thirds. The subject should normally be supported by secondary mass or colour and distant or out of focus mass or colour. The space planned for the design area should incorporate all three depths of field with approximately one third devoted to the centre of interest and one third to negative space with the remaining third being used for the supporting areas. The line of design is the direction which the eye follows as it winds its way through the pattern. It should twist or curve upon itself and not lead the viewer out of the painted area. The direction a line takes can indicate motion and strength, e.g. a vertical line indicates strength while a slanting line indicates action. A horizontal line is restful and a jagged line indicates restlessness. A curved line is usually peaceful and rhythmical.

Proportion is another important area which is often neglected. The design should suit the vehicle on which it is to be painted and once again space is to be considered. The subject matter should be drawn to *scale*, ie leaves and the accompanying blossoms should be suited to each other and two or more blossoms of varying sizes should be drawn according to their natural state, e.g. violets would not be the same size as daffodils in the same painting (unless it was a field scene and violets were in the foreground and daffodils in the distance). *Relative size* is important. *Colour* is a visual sensation which arouses emotion. (*See* Colour.) *Texture* is both visual and tactile and should be appropriate for the design. *Balance* is usually attained by planning space and positioning subject matter. A large mass may be counter balanced by two smaller masses, or a 'deep' area by two lighter 'deep' areas elsewhere. The painting should be able to be viewed from any angle and be pleasing to the eye. *Dominance* is the effect the centre of interest would have over the rest of the design. *Contrast* is essential in all areas of design to add interest and give variety. No two lines should be identical or follow the same path, no two flowers should face the same way, variety of colour will help. The *elements* of a design are *colour, tone, texture, line, size* and *shape*. Each of these elements should exhibit the following *principles*: *dominance, harmony, contrast, balance, repetition* and *gradation*. Look for lack of balance, lines leading into corners, out of the 'frame', at right angles, disassociation of various areas, lack of proportion and lack of depth or third dimension.

Elements of Design Checklist

	Dominance	Harmony	Contrast	Balance	Repetition	Gradation
Colour						
Tone						
Texture						
Line						
Size						
Shape						

Each time you paint your pieces use the above check list to see if you have all of the fundamental bases of design listed in the horizontal column for all of the subjects listed in the vertical column.

(And do not forget to check your 'Rule of Threes' at the same time.)

Three colours for each area of painted space, leaf, petal, meadow, trunk of tree or wall.

Three values of colour, and three areas of strength and weakness.

Small, medium and large areas of each colour and small medium and large areas of both colour and design.

Original colour, shaded colour and reflected colour.

Foreground, middleground and background.

Highlight, shadow and reflected light.

Areas in strong light 'washed out', areas in unlit foreground in focus and support areas slightly out of focus.

Art nouveau Decorative style of painting from late 19th century. Taken from folk art, plant forms, etc.

Ash Residue from bones which provides some of the chemicals used in glazes: silica, alumina, potash, iron, magnesia, phosphorus and lime. A source of flux.

Asphaltum Liquid tar or pitch which is used as a 'resist' when etching china and glass.

Aufsetweiss European enamel.

Background The supporting area for the focal point or centre of interest in the design. It is used to give an illusion of depth and natural elements as well as providing contrast for the subject. A background for a wipe out painting is applied by laying different colours on in patches with broad sweeps of varying length in appropriate places. For example, paint pink for a rose theme where you might want your pink rose to be, paint less of the same colour a little away from that area for a supporting blossom and add more for reflection elsewhere in the design. Now add some blue and green in patches which vary in size around your pink area, going over it in a couple of places, draw the colour out along your line of design, keeping close to it. Do not drag the heavier applications of colour out into the distant background areas as you will lose your design line and the work will spread, tempting you to fill it up with masses of design and colour which will detract from your centre of interest. For this distant background area, use lighter shades and tones of your chosen colour scheme. Place other colours for interest and, if you know where you want it, place some dark colour with a little of the pink or blue etc added to it to soften it. These strokes should be applied with *cross-hatching*, that is, a couple of broad flat strokes in one direction and another one or two strokes crossing the first two as an 'X'. A pattern of these strokes will give you varying degrees of colour with, hopefully, *windows of light* which you will, once again hopefully, leave alone. The applied background is now blended by *filtering* or *feathering*, very light brush strokes which gently move the paint, blending and merging the colours without losing them. The heavier application of paint near the focal point is softened and merged with the lighter background. (*Exercise*: Paint an area heavily with a light colour, so that you can see the brushstrokes, then load your brush with a darker colour and feather the first application to blend the ridges and visible brush strokes *without leaving dark paint* on them. It *is* possible!) To give the illusion of *shadows*, grey your original colours and apply soft indistinct brushstrokes in the rough shape of a leaf or other subject. This can be done in the wet paint, over fired paint, wiped out of or shaped up with wet paint over fired paint or any combination of these techniques.

'Back to front'   Painting what would be physically at the back of the scene, eg the mountains, first, then the middle ground and then the foreground so that the closest part of the scene sits happily on the background. Not always easy for a beginner to do.

Balance   The design should be positioned on the porcelain so as to be pleasing to the eye, which should be able to follow the line of design around and within the porcelain shape. A design which is top heavy will keep the eye of the viewer on that part and the remaining painting will be ignored.

Ball clay   Fine plastic clay used in the making of porcelain as a plasticiser.

Ball mill   A jar filled with smooth stones or pebbles which, when turned, is used to fine grind powdered glazes.

Balsam of copaiba   An oil from South America which is used as a medium. Usually combined with other oils because of its fast drying action.

Banding Placing a band around the edge of a plate or drinking vessel, usually with the aid of a banding wheel.

Banding wheel Tool used to turn plates, vases etc to allow a band or circular design to be applied. A record player or Lazy Susan may be substituted. Centre the plate on the wheel and spin to see if it is 'true'. Fix in position with Blue Tack or plasticine. Dip a square shader in turpentine and paint and, with the plate spinning gently, hold the brush in position around the outer border. Continue towards the centre of the plate. A design painted in different colours and varying widths will make an interesting background for 'wipe out' florals. Another experiment is to lay paint fairly thickly on the plate, either on the spinning banding wheel or on a still plate and then place it on the banding wheel. Dribble turpentine and spin the plate rapidly to force the turpentine into rivulets through the paint.

Baroque An art style of the 17th and 18th centuries, initially deliberately deformed or distorted figures or objects, frequently with ambiguous intent. The classic rules of art were broken to emphasise the emotion and provoke a response in the viewer.

Base for raised gold White powder, similar in final appearance to enamel and not to be confused with raised paste. I find this an excellent texture paste which can be mixed with almost any liquid and which will withstand several fires. It may be coloured with the addition of a very small amount of powder paint and will tolerate foreign matter such as glass, sand etc. Applied over wet paint, it will absorb some of the colour. *See* Carey's products.

Bases A term used for a flux which causes the glaze to become fusible. The chemicals which make up a glaze formula consist of acids, bases and neutrals. Alkalis and alkali earths are bases and the most common ones used are the oxides of barium, calcium, lead, lithium, magnesium, potassium, sodium, strontium and zinc.

Bas relief Low relief sculpture which only slightly projects from the surface and with no part of the design undercut.

Belleek Irish porcelain ware with iridescent pearly glaze. American Belleek is soft paste porcelain with an ivory colour.

Biomorphic shapes Shapes and designs which are based on organic life.

Bisque 1. Clay which has been fired at a low temperature sufficient to harden the body for handling but retain porosity to allow it to absorb a glaze.
2. Clay which has been fired to maturity but not glazed. Unglazed chinaware may be painted.
Underglaze painting: the design is painted with oxides or paint pigments,

allowed to dry and the painted object is dipped in glaze and fired. For *bisque painting* matt colours are used, as fluxed colours would be glossy on the matt surface but not with their usual even brilliance. Matt colours are available, however to matt your normal colours mix ¼ to ½ parts of zinc oxide to 1 part of paint and make a stiff paste with grinding oil. Lavender oil is used as a painting medium. Porcelain bisque should be smooth, fine grained and waterproof. It is possible to fine sand coarser bisqueware. To paint on bisque, prepare a basic palette of light, medium and dark colours plus white which is used for highlights. Sketch the design with a lead pencil and, using lavender oil as medium, softly paint in design. Wipe out highlights immediately as the porous surface makes this difficult. Use the lavender oil to clean brushes between colours. Paint the subject first then the background, feathering out into the negative space areas as the paint dries rapidly. Unwanted areas may be erased with the lavender oil. A second coat of paint may be added when dry and before firing because of the porous nature of the clay body. More detail, depth and colour may be applied using a very dry brush. Add highlights with white paint and place shadows and interesting brushstrokes. Fire at 700°C. A higher fire will tend to gloss the matt colours. Liquid Bright Gold is good for decoration—fires matt. Enamel paste or penwork scrolling all enhance the bisque ware when done well. Bisque may be 'grounded' by applying a colour heavily and smoothly. It is sometimes possible to remove fired paint from bisque by soaking in vinegar overnight.

Bisque eggs   Painted as for bisque china.

Black   A porcelain colour derived from some of the following: cobalt, chromium, copper, iron and manganese. Care should be taken not to apply it too thickly as it will chip off particularly when used in pen or line work. It is sometimes used to shade a colour and once again should be used cautiously to prevent 'dirtying' the colour. Works well when softened or greyed with blues or purples. When mixed with yellow, will give an interesting green.

Black spot   A mildew-like spot which appears after firing, caused by low firing at bisque stage. Fire hot; paint and fire again.

Blanc de Chine   French terminology for white glazed Chinese porcelain.

Blanks   The porcelain shapes before they are painted.

Blend   1. Mix two or more substances such as oil and paint pigments. 2. To move applied colour while still wet by 'filtering' or with light brush strokes.

Blistering   A blister effect in the glaze caused in firing.

Blocking in   The application of paint in broad flat strokes within a previously sketched or designated area.

Blue A porcelain painting colour derived from cobalt. A lot of blues require the additon of a little flux to help them mature.

Blushing To rub mixed paint into the design with your finger or a pad to tint it. E.g. dampen the tip of your finger with medium and pick up a little Blood Red. Gently rub the design with the colour and give it a blush of pink. Do not use too much colour.

Body The clay used in making the porcelain object.

Boiling Blisters or craters forming on the glaze after firing at a temperature too high for the soft glazes.

Bone china Fine semi-translucent earthenware containing kaolin and calcified bones which resembles porcelain. The high proportion of bone ash (40%) lowers the melting point of the clay.

Bordering A term used when airbrushing. The paint becomes darker towards the edge of the object being painted. This effect may be obtained either by a heavier application of paint towards the edge or the use of a darker shade or colour.

Broken colour Initially a term used by French Impressionists to describe the application of various colours in separate short crosshatched strokes to give the optical illusion of blended colour.

Brush cleaner Product available from Carey's to clean brushes.

Brushes Our most useful and often most necessary tools and probably those for which we have the least respect and which cost the most! Brushes come in many different varieties and are usually made from the bristles and hairs of animals. Squirrel hair from various parts of the world, sable fur, fitch, skunk, badger, goat, camel etc. There are some synthetic brushes used as well but these do not seem to have the flexibility of natural fur.

Square shader A straight tipped flat brush varying in width from one millimetre to several centimetres. Used for washes of colour, shaded loads, cross hatching etc. The hairs are both short or medium in length.

Pointed shader A full bodied pointed brush used in European or Dresden style painting. Used also for strong line work, shaded strokes and painting in a design.

Liner A fine slender pointed brush used for delicate lines and fine detail.

Scroller A long slender pointed brush used for lines and scrolls.

Long scroller Long slender scroller.

Square quill A full rounded brush with a blunt end.

Mop brush Very large soft haired brush used for dusting.

Mini liner Long very fine liner.

Long liner A little shorter than a scroller.

Cat's tongue Long flat liner.

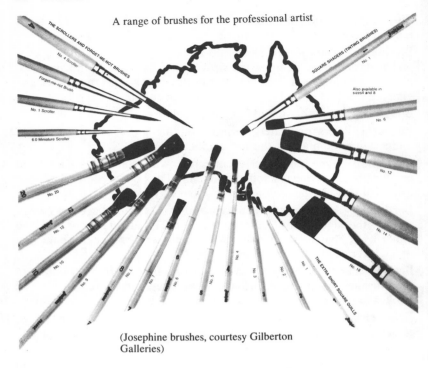

A range of brushes for the professional artist

(Josephine brushes, courtesy Gilberton Galleries)

A variety of square shaders (Courtesy Carey's Products)

Flo-line brush A long haired brush with a full body which tapers down to a very fine point.

Stippler A flat based brush either square or angled (deerfoot) which comes in various sizes from about 2 millimetres in diameter to about a centimetre. Used dry to blend wet paint for foliage and stippled effect.

Deerfoot stippler Flat based, angled brush for stippling.

Berry brush Short full pointed brush.

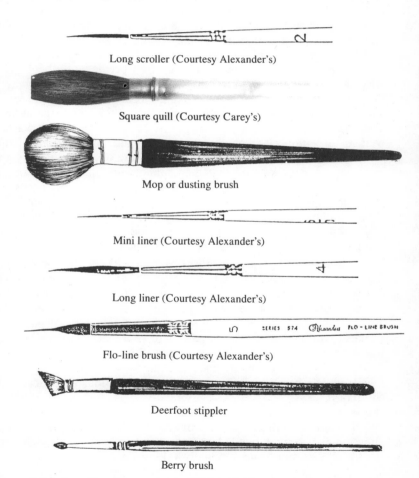

Long scroller (Courtesy Alexander's)

Square quill (Courtesy Carey's)

Mop or dusting brush

Mini liner (Courtesy Alexander's)

Long liner (Courtesy Alexander's)

Flo-line brush (Courtesy Alexander's)

Deerfoot stippler

Berry brush

Care of brushes. Brushes are expensive! With careful use they will last a long time. Here are a few general rules for care. Remember the hairs in a natural brush come from an animal and are similar in structure to your own hair. Always buy good quality brushes which suit your needs and depending on your likes and dislikes, long or short haired brushes, full or fine. A long haired full bodied brush is usually more flexible and carries more paint than the short haired variety. Do not bend a brush when the hairs are still stiff from lack of use (or care). Dip in turpentine or oil first and allow to soften. Do not bend a brush harshly at the ferrule. The hairs will break. Do not stab your brush either into the jar of turpentine or onto your plate. If you would like a stippled effect for fur or foliage keep an old brush for this purpose. Do not discard all old brushes. There are a number of uses to which they can be put: Applying resists and textures, cleaning, painting on a 'toothed' surface; the handles may be used as a tool or holder for a pen nib or quill ferrule. Do not stand your brushes on their painting tips as this will result in a permanently bent shape. Also do not stand them for great lengths of time the other way as this allows the oil, turpentine and paint, dirt etc to run into the ferrule and cause the hairs to separate. If you are not going to paint for a time, place all your brushes flat in a covered container after first washing well in turpentine, then methylated spirits and finally in an oil like lavender oil to keep them supple. Once they are oiled, pull them gently into shape and make sure that they cannot subsequently be jammed against anything which will cause them to bend. To expel excess oil, place the hairs on a lint free cloth and gently press with your finger. Do not pull on the hairs as they are only glued in. Washing occasionally with soap and water or a shampoo is good but make sure they are completely dry and oiled again before painting.

Brushstrokes   Conventional brushstrokes are like scales for a pianist. They should be practised and used skilfully as 'paint is applied with one stroke and removed with the next'. If you can make your brushstrokes work for you, your painting will not be overworked or muddy. However, for individual work do not follow a set pattern of strokes to form a leaf, flower or pattern or your leaf, flower and pattern will be the same as everyone else's leaf, flower and pattern. Brushes should be conditioned before each painting session.

Flat load The brush has an even coat of one colour right across the width of it.

Shaded load The brush is loaded with paint in a circular motion, going into the mound of mixed paint (from right to left in an anti-clockwise direction for a right handed person; left handers left to right in a clockwise direction) and gradually taking up paint. The stroke will apply a heavier application of paint on the left side (right side for left handers) shaded to the right (left) with a lighter colour tone.

Side load Only one side of the brush is loaded.

Mixed load When two or more colours are loaded onto the brush usually with the shaded load or side load technique.

Straight strokes Pull the loaded brush towards yourself. Vary the length of the strokes. Used for backgrounds, washes, cross-hatching and tints.

Comma stroke The loaded brush is held at a forty-five degree angle and pulled towards the painter in the shape of a 'C', either short or long, back to front or normally. Pressure is applied to the brush at the top of the stroke and lifted as the stroke is executed. An elongated comma stroke will give a long tail effect. Used to frame and cut in.

Dash A fully loaded brush is used on its tip so that a narrow band of colour is applied. Useful for branches, veins etc.

There are obviously many positions for your brushes which you will discover by experiment or accident. Use as many as you can to become versatile.

Build-up A line of paint caused by too much paint or oil on the brush, inexpert application or grainy paints.

Burnish To rub Roman Gold or burnishing gold with a burnishing cloth, burnishing sand, or fibre-glass brush to give it a rich satin finish. The best results are obtained when this is done while the piece is still warm from the kiln.

Burnishing gold Most golds, other than Liquid Bright Gold have to be burnished. Made from pure metal from which the alloys have been removed. *See* individual names such as Roman Gold, Fluxed and Unfluxed Gold.

Cache-pot Small lidded dish.

Cadmium Element used in some very bright reds. Should only be fired once at a very low temperature eg 700°C after all other painting has been completed.

Calcine Chemicals reduced to powder with heat.

Calligraphy Formal script written with a pen or brush.

Calyx Outer protective envelope of flower.

Calyx—consisting of **sepals**

Camaieu   French terminology for monochrome painting.

Cameo   Small piece of relief carving, usually in two layers, the lower one a contrasting colour to form a contrasting base for the relief layer.

Camieu   French terminology for silhouette painting.

Candles   It is possible to paint on candles as you would on soap. Also on waxed surfaces such as the inside of a milk carton, waxed paper and plasticised surfaces, although all these surfaces tend to show scratch marks. Using a fast drying medium, paint as though on china. May be initially sprayed with hairspray and then with a craft lacquer to preserve. The aerosol cans seem to be better as it may be possible to move the paint with a brushed on sealer.

Canvas porcelain   Very thin porcelain (1-2 millimetres thick) which is given the name of porcelain canvas. It is slightly rough in texture with a matt surface and is usually only available in comparatively small 'tiles'. The rough surface or tooth is hard on brushes and paints will not fire evenly as a rule, so the use of a matt art varnish spray when the work is completed is advisable. There is sometimes a difference in the two sides but it does not really matter which one is used for painting. Normal porcelain paints are used and the pieces are fired either flat or supported in an upright position. As they are slightly transparent, an interesting effect is obtained when they are lit from the back.

Carbon paper   Used to make a copy of the study. If you must do this, and it is necessary for some subjects and for some beginners, try graphite paper.

Cartouche   Framed ornamental panel with symbols or inscriptions.

Casting   Forming a shape by pouring liquid clay into a plaster mould.

Cast shadow   Shadow thrown by object.

Cement   For mending china. Enamel or white relief mixed with a little flux may be painted onto a broken edge and fired low. The piece to be mended may need support during the firing. There are commercial cements available and the manufacturers' instructions should be followed.

Centre of interest   The focal point or that part of your design which should leap to the fore when first viewed.

Ceramic à froid   A solvent based ceramic liquid colour which may be applied to a porcelain surface (or any other surface such as glass, metal, leather, wood, etc.) and which has the appearance of fired porcelain. It will set hard in 24 hours. There are 22 colours which are intermixable. White spirit is used as a diluent. The ceramic paint may be applied with a brush, by print method or, for a very effective decoration, a few drops of various colours may be floated on the surface of a basin of water. The colours will mix and swirl together and create complex patterns. The object to be painted is dipped into the solution and withdrawn immediately and allowed to dry. It takes a little experimenting but the results are a lot of fun.

There is a clear glaze, a filler undercoat and a thinner which may be obtained to go with these unfired ceramics.

Ceramic à l'eau A water based ceramic liquid colour similar to Ceramic à Froid but which may be hardened at 200°C. There are 10 colours which are diluted with water.

Ceramics General term to cover various clay bodies.

Chamois May be used for padding and for rubbing gold with sand.

Chelsea paper Art paper for oil painting. To paint on Chelsea paper, coat first with medium and rapidly paint design. Dry and paint again, two or three times. May be cleaned with turpentine. Spray with Chelsea Spray.

Chiaroscuro *Chiaro-ascuro*. The exaggerated treatment of light and shade as contrast in art.

China General term applied to white porcelain ware. May be Japanese, European or American. European china may be Limoges, Bavarian or Caverswall bone china from England.

China clay Kaolin, a fine white clay used as an absorbent and filler in ceramics.

China mist Paint in an aerosol can in a range of colours. Used to tint a surface by spraying lightly and firing at 018 or 715°C. Several applications are used for darker background work as heavy coats will chip off. May be used for bisque and glass; however, with glass, light applications only and fired low as for glass between each application. May be sprayed over fired Liquid Bright Gold to matt it with any one of several colours.

Chinoiserie French terminology for Oriental style work.

Chroma Intensity or brightness/dullness of a colour. A greyed colour loses its chroma or intensity. The brighter the colour, the greater the impact and therefore to be used less.

Chrome colours Blues and greens.

Circular lines Applied either by:
1. using a banding wheel,
2. holding the pencil in the normal grip and using a finger held against the edge of the plate as a guide and rotating the plate. The pencil automatically marks the circle. The innermost line is drawn first if more than one is required.
3. using a length of cotton or string attached to a pin embedded into plasticine or Blue Tack positioned in the centre of the plate and a

pencil attached to the other end. By varying the length of the string, the lines can be spaced as desired,

4. using a small tool roughly triangular in shape with carefully positioned holes and a hooked end which holds the tool to the edge of the plate.

Classical Art based on the Greek and Roman principles of art. Characterised by a controlled rational observance of the accepted rules and styles.

Clay Stiff viscous earth consisting mainly of aluminium silicate which, when mixed with water, forms a pliable paste. It is formed by the decomposition of feldspars, a component of granite. Kaolin is an example of pure clay. The main characteristics of clay include:

Porosity Sand or grog is mixed with clay to allow the water to evaporate.

Shrinkage The clay particles form a tighter bond with the evaporation of water.

Vitreousness The clay is rendered impervious to water by the exposure to high temperatures.

Plasticity Clay is pliable and may be moulded at the direction of the artist. The degree of plasticity is determined by the water content, the presence of organic matter and the size of the clay particles.

There are three main types of clay used by ceramists. *Earthenware,* which is comparatively low fired porous clay, *stoneware,* a hard dense ware which may be fired higher than earthenware and because of this is quite vitreous, and *porcelain,* the hardest and finest of the clay products. The sequence of texture in the clay is as follows. Initially the clay is malleable and may be formed into a shape. If left to dry, it becomes leather hard and may be still gently coaxed into slight changes of form or carved and trimmed. It eventually becomes bone dry and may no longer be adapted without cracking or breaking. If it is then fired low enough to simply harden but still remain porous, it is termed bisque and will accept an application of glaze. It is also called bisque if it is fired to maturity and left unglazed. The final step is to glaze the ware and fire to maturity.

Clock divider A pattern to divide a clock into equal segments.

Cloisonne Design outlined in metal and flooded with enamel. It is possible to create an interesting facsimile using enamel pastes and gold penwork.

Closed A term used to describe a fast drying medium.

Clove oil An oil which slows the drying process of the medium and keeps it 'open'.

Cobalt colours Dark blues. Mix with most colours.

Collage The additional decoration of various materials which are attached to a (painted) surface.

Colour Colour has three dimensions, *hue, value* and *intensity. Hue is the name given to a colour; value* is the lightness or darkness of a colour and *intensity* is the brightness or strength of a colour. A colour which is lightened by the addition of white is called a *tint* and if a colour is darkened with the addition of black it is called a *shade.* A tint has a lighter value than the hue used to make it.

Cool colours are usually blues and green and *warm* colours reds and yellows. However, each hue may have a warm and a cool appearance with the addition of one of the primary colours, eg a blue green is cool whereas a yellow green is warm.

Monochrome The various tints and shades of one hue.

Analogous Neighbouring colours on the colour wheel.

Complementary Opposite colours on the colour wheel.

Split complementary One colour plus two colours which are adjacent to its complement.

Triadic Any three colours equally distant on the colour wheel.

Sympathetic and *harmonious* A primary colour with some adjacent colours.

Colour contrast Usually colours opposite each other on the colour wheel, e.g.: yellow/violet; red/green; orange/blue.

Colour perspective Distant colours are greyer and lighter while close colours are brighter and more intense.

Colour scheme Combination of colours.

Colour spectrum Violet, indigo, blue, green, yellow, orange and red.

Colour wheel A colour chart showing primary, secondary and tertiary colours and the various colour combinations which are traditionally most pleasing.

Comma stroke A useful stroke in the shape of a comma which, with a square shader, surrounds, cuts in and places backgrounds and, with a liner, scrolls and enamelling.

Complementary *Direct complementary* Colours immediately opposite each other on a colour wheel: black and white; red and green; blue and yellow; and orange and purple. *See* diagram on page 28.

Double complementary Two pairs of colours on a colour wheel.

Composition The formation of a pattern or design which should harmonise with the blank porcelain to give a pleasing result. There must be a theme which has a focal point, with supporting design and a gradual blend with the white or neutrally coloured background. There should be variety in form, colour and design to provide interest. There should always be a suggestion or 'surprise', usually an understated echo of the theme which attracts the eye of the viewer but does not detract from the focal point. General rules are that the lines of the design should follow the outline of the object being painted, the main

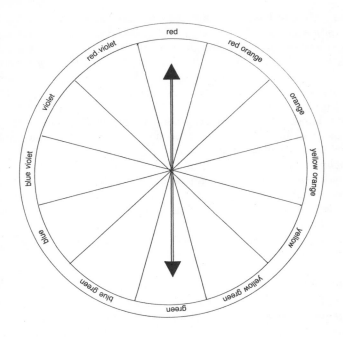

Colour wheel showing direct complementary colours

portion of the design should be contained within a triangle and 'three' is the order of the day. Three main flowers in a floral design, three major points of intense depth, three areas of design: focal point, secondary supporting group and tertiary area or background. Three areas of colour: small, medium and large; and three shades of colour. These are conventional guidelines and as always, there are exceptions. Obvious faults are lines at right angles to a curve, too 'busy' a design, background features dominating the scene. A good test is to walk away from the painting and return to it later. If your eye immediately goes to a part of the design other than the focal area, that part is usually at fault in some way.

Concave   Indented or curved inwards.

Conditioning brushes   Brushes, like good cooking utensils, have to be conditioned in order to work efficiently. The first time you use a brush each painting session, initially dip it into your medium almost to the ferrule. Using your tile, work the oil through the hairs of the brush by drawing it along the tile and fanning out the fibres. Re-shape the tip with your fingers and gently press all the oil out of it with one of your fingers against the tile. Re-load the brush by dipping it into the medium approximately half the length of its hairs, wipe the excess oil off on the edge of the jar and gently press any further surplus out before loading the brush with paint.

Cones Cones are small white pyramids of clay to which flux has been added and which melt at varying temperatures. They are used to give you the time/temperature curve of firing time when using your kiln. They may also be used to test the heat and accuracy of your kiln. The time taken to bring your kiln to a certain temperature is important to the reaction of the paints and other substances painted on the glazed surface. The longer a kiln takes to reach a certain temperature, the less heat is required to mature the paint and a cone will indicate this more accurately than a thermometer which merely indicates the internal temperature of the kiln. That is to say the longer your kiln takes to fire, the lower the temperature at which the cone melts. When exposed to the heat for less time in a rapid fire the cone needs a higher temperature to cause it to bend. The length of time taken to reach a desired temperature in the kiln is frequently governed by the amount it contains or the efficiency of the power supply. Cones give a truer reading of the effect the heat has on the clay body of the pieces being fired. The melting point of the cones and the rate of degrees per hour is indicated by the manufacturer on the container in which they come. The scale below is therefore only a guide.

Cone	Fahrenheit	Centigrade
022	1110	598
021	1135	612
020	1175	635
019	1260	682
018	1320	715
017	1375	746
016	1455	790
015	1475	801
014	1540	837
013	1560	848
012	1620	882
011	1640	893
010	1665	907
09	1690	921
08	1750	954
07	1800	982
06	1845	1007
05	1915	1046
04	1940	1060
03	2000	1093
02	2040	1115
01	2080	1137

Contrast   Striking difference. The use of contrast in painting adds interest and relieves boredom. Check the following areas to see if you have contrast and with it curiosity for your viewers in your painting: Lights against darks, straight and curved lines with wide and narrow areas, distinct regions and blurred 'out of focus' regions, clear colour and greyed colour, the obvious and the suggested, contrast in shape such as well defined shapes and suggested shapes, rough and smooth areas, full face and turned blossoms, painted or positive areas for opposition to negative space or vacant areas. Keep in mind that the opposites on the colour wheel will heighten the impact of each other when placed side by side. Do not overlook the strength of a sharp, clear design on pure white porcelain or the richness of a ground border with a delicate pattern.

Contrast varnish   Organic colour solution from Degussa to assist with even application of gold. It fires off in the kiln and does not affect gold finish.

Conventional design   Traditional semi-stylised naturalistic design.

Convex   Outwardly curved.

Cool colours   Blues, violets and greens which give the appearance of cool, receding and background colours. A wash of blue over a dominant secondary feature will force it into the background. Yellow greens are in the warm range of colours.

Copper enamel   May be used with caution on porcelain. It is best used on a prepared surface, such as one from which the glaze has been removed or to which one of the texture pastes or structural substances has been added. Very small amounts of the powdered enamel sprinkled onto the glaze will not chip off, however larger quantities may, if not in the cooling process then at an embarrassing later date. There are several types of copper enamel available: a powder form, which is either opaque or transparent, and solid rods and shapes of coloured enamel. All these forms come in a range of colours which may be mixed together. The powder form may be mixed with any of the oil based mediums, glycerine or waterbased mediums, milk, or simple syrups such as coca-cola. If applied with flux it will melt more readily and flow onto your work. As with most of these substances which have so many variables, the result is quite unpredictable and almost always interesting, although it could be unattractive if overdone. Moderation in all things!

Cornelli scrolling   Snail-like trailing over the surface of the porcelain in coloured or gold penwork, raised paste or enamel.

Corolla   The cup of petals which forms the inner and usually most colourful part of a flower.

Correction of fired errors There are a number of ways to correct, hide or disguise errors or bad workmanship fired into the porcelain. Ingenuity!

Chipped edge Incorporate a pattern of textured design into the area and build up the broken space gradually with one of the more reliable textured pastes in a succession of low firings and then paint the area with either gold, platinum or one of the metallic powders. Another idea is to frame it in a slightly smaller frame.

Too busy a design Portion of the design may be covered with one of the texture pastes, acid look or the glaze chipped away with glass excising. *Or* accentuate the design with a dramatic background fire and dust the whole area, leaving some of the original area lightly covered and pen the outline and part of the background. The remaining design becomes shadows. *Use* Rustiban to remove most of the design, lustre and penwork to develop and highlight what is left. Pen and flooded enamel is sometimes helpful. If the piece is already ruined, experiment!

Covercoat Water soluble liquid which dries to form a plastic film which is used to protect or mask an area of porcelain. It peels off easily once it has served its purpose.

Craft knife There are many uses for this handy scalpel-like tool. Cutting into 'resists' for sharp detail, cleaning up gold which has extended over the edge of paste and borders and cutting out plasticised clay for moulding are just a few of the obvious ones.

Crawling Where the glaze has pulled away from the body of the clay and formed into little heaps. Probably caused by the glaze being applied to unclean bisque. An interesting effect when deliberately caused with texture pastes.

Crazing A network of surface cracks which appears in the glaze. Occasionally caused deliberately by the manufacturer but usually caused by the glaze and body of the piece expanding at different temperatures and causing stress fractures in the glaze.

Crest Coat of arms.

Cross hatching Application of paint with brushstrokes which cross over in a grid or diamond pattern. These may be straight or curved to show a contour. The applied paint is then feathered and blended into a smooth, even application with the lighter and heavier patches of colour giving variation of tones and values. Highlights are left in place and look quite natural.

Crystal clear glaze White powder which contains flux and which is used to dust onto a piece of porcelain to give it a high gloss. It will eat out some colours so caution is advised when using it.

Damar varnish   For use with raised paste to facilitate the making of long scrolls.

Decals   Transfers with designs to be applied to china. Wet the decal for a few seconds and apply it in the desired position. Gently press out any air bubbles and remove backing which should just slide off. Allow to dry thoroughly. Fire at a medium temperature. 780–800°C. It is possible to obtain gold borders to fit various sized plates. Follow the manufacturers' instructions.

Decorate   To embellish or enhance beauty. Porcelain is traditionally already beautiful with its pure white translucent glaze and rounded forms.

Decorative design   A design applied to enhance and decorate an otherwise plain object.

Deerfoot blender   Stippling brush in graduated sizes with an angled base.

Degussa   *See* Degussa Products.

Dehydration   During the initial firing of clay, the water is drawn from the clay during the firing range 150–600°C and it is necessary to vent the kiln to allow the steam generated to escape. Firing should be slow during this period to prevent a build up of steam resulting in cracking and perhaps explosion of the clay bodies.

Delft   Tin glazed earthenware from Holland, usually blue and white but may be any colour.

Demonstrate   To show how something is done. Frequently we are asked to demonstrate and there are one or two points which will help both the audience and the demonstrator. Firstly, choose a sufficiently large surface on which to paint or demonstrate so that all may see it. If you are standing in front of your audience, do not clutch this surface to your chest. Try to learn to paint from either side or literally with the back of the plate or tile to your chest and your painting hand in front and to the bottom, so that your fans can see what you are doing. If you are sitting at a table, do not hunch over your work. Describe and discuss your subject first and when it is time to paint, do so slowly, explaining why you are doing what you are doing, how you are doing it, which colours and tools you are using and what you hope to achieve. Try to keep talking all the time, even when you are also trying to concentrate and remember to use stronger colours and heavier loads if in a large room with a large audience. Try not to be boastful, remember, people can actually see how good you are! Do not discuss other teachers and teaching methods in a derogatory fashion and if things are not going well do not look for excuses. Try to assess the reactions of your group and do not be disconcerted by late comers or the lady asleep in the front row! Audiences have a

Brushstrokes

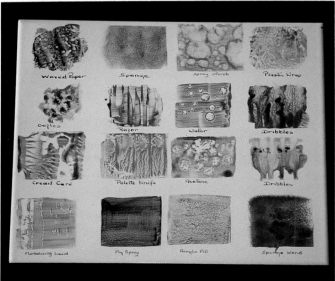

Fun with wet paint—The paint was either pressed, padded or dampened with various tools and solutions.

1st row: Waxed paper, sponge, spray starch, plastic wrap.
2nd row: 'Ooples' with turpentine, razor, water, dribbles and runs.

3rd row: Credit card, palette knife, acetone and more dribbles.
4th row: Marbelizing liquid (yes, for lustre), flyspray, acrylic fill and sponge.

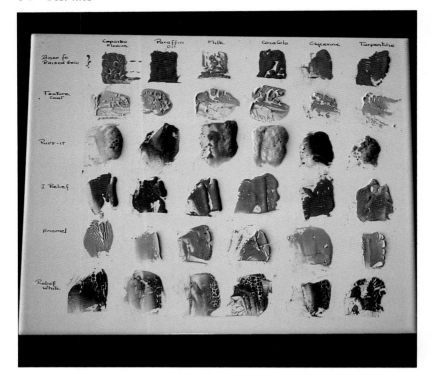

Test Tile of Pastes: All substances were mixed to a fairly stiff consistency, dried overnight on a ceramic tile, fired very slowly to 800°C, in my kiln. None of the substances chipped off in the first fire and would not be expected to on a ceramic tile. All were shiny with the exception of Ruff It.

Base for Raised Gold: Copaiba Medium—flattened just a little, interesting separation; Paraffin—no separation, slightly flat uninteresting blob; Milk—interesting separation; Coca Cola—little separation; Glycerine—flatter, otherwise no change; Turpentine—very little separation.

Texture Coat: Very interesting separation with all mediums.

I Relief: Smooth, slightly flattened surface with very little separation with all liquids.

Enamel (Fay Good's Dresden): Copaiba Medium—very interesting striated separation; Paraffin, Milk, Coca Cola—retained height with a small amount of separation; Glycerine—flat; Turpentine—interesting separation.

Relief White: Most interesting of all—good separation with various shapes with all mediums.

Remember: It is impossible to predict accurately the results of texture because the amount of liquid added, colour added, china on which it is placed, thickness of application and time/temperature curve all have an effect on the final result.

limited attention span so try to think up some surprises to relieve any monotony. Try to answer all questions; however, do not be afraid to say you do not know but that you will find out. Keep in mind that people have come to see you not to criticise you.

Depth A field of depth or distance from front to back to your design, a three dimensional effect created by shading.

Design Sketch for a work of art. The elements of a good design are *line, direction, shape, value, colour, texture, size* and a lot of intuitive sense. The plate or any round shape is one of the most difficult to design. The line of design is usually an S or C curve, or reverse of these, and this line should take into account the shape and form of the piece, and be proportionate in size. There should be large, medium and small areas of mass with the subject matter in series of uneven numbers, threes, fives etc, and covering no more than two thirds of the area. This leaves at least one third *negative space*, which is also broken into interesting areas of differing sizes. All design rules may at times be broken and as always there are happy accidents. The guidelines for design are just that . . . guidelines to be followed where appropriate. So the following are suggestions only.

Place the focal mass on the largest area of porcelain, slightly off centre with the centre of interest also to one side of the mass. Design lines should curve round and if an imaginary line is followed it will lead back to the focal area. Lines should not lead into corners, into the centre of the frame, or divide the area in half. No two lines should meet in the centre.

If the design is floral, no two flowers should be face to face or back to back, nor should any two or three form a row. The flow of design indicates the direction the eye should follow. The focal point is emphasised by the more subdued supporting and surrounding areas. And no area should completely encircle another.

Once your design is complete, rotate it. It should be pleasing from all angles. Faults in design are sometimes obvious in a mirror and often more obvious after leaving the painting for some time. One frequently becomes so involved with each individual portion that it is impossible to see the 'whole'.

Diaper All over surface decoration in a simple repeat pattern of squares or diamonds.

Diluent A liquid used to dilute or thin down a substance.

Dimension values To give the illusion of depth.

Dipping The act of submerging the object you are painting into a solution.

1. Float a small amount of different coloured lustres on water (incidentally, it is rumoured that lustres will sink if they are no longer

any good, however I have successfully used a sunken lustre). Submerge a porcelain blank and allow the lustres to adhere to its surface. Remove and allow to dry. Fire. Paint mixed with oil may be applied in the same manner however the result is not as effective.

2. Submerge into acid to etch. *Caution with acid.*

Diptych Painting or relief sculpture in two panels.

Direct complement Two opposing colours on a colour wheel.

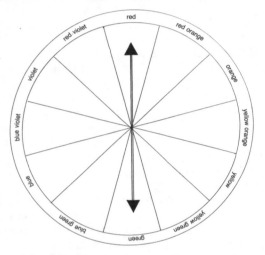

Colour wheel showing direct complementary colours

Dishwashing detergent Powder paint mixed with detergent produces interesting effects—matt when fired and the bubbles leave an unusual pattern.

Dividers A drawing instrument which may be used for accurate measurement. The distance between eyes, lines and other focal points can be measured on the study and checked on your drawing. An invaluable tool for portraits and wildlife painting.

Dominance The quality of that part of the design which is the focal point. Unfortunately we frequently cause a minor part of the design to be a dominant factor.

Dots Dots are used for decoration and may be either penwork or paste. For paste dots, take a nib or stylus and push into a mound of mixed paste so that the paste sits on the top of the tool. Gently touch the paste to the surface to be decorated and lift again, pulling away in a circular motion until the dot is the desired size. For a diminishing line of dots, do not reload with paste as you would for identical dots.

Pointillism is the art of creating a design or picture by painting it entirely in dots which vary in size, colour and density.

Double complement   Two pairs of opposing colours on a colour wheel.

Dovia paper   Plasticised paper on which you may paint with porcelain paints and Copaiba based or fast drying oils. Same techniques etc, except that it obviously is not fired! May be cleaned off with turpentine.

Drapery   The name given to clothing worn by the figures in a painting, fabrics in background and also to the clothing on figurines.
Lace drapery is the name given to net or lace dipped in porcelain slip and used to dress figurines.

Drawing   Sketching with a pencil. Doodling is good practice. A few exercises follow which will help you develop an 'eye' and a 'hand'. Have pen and paper always handy and whenever you have a moment, play practice.
1. Select an object and do not remove your gaze from it while you reproduce it without lifting the pen from the paper. This is contour drawing.
2. Turn an object upside down and draw it. The unfamiliar shape will confuse your preconceived notions.
3. Draw the negative space and identify your subject or ask someone else to do so.
4. Draw something while you are looking at it then draw it from memory.

Dresden   A fine hard bodied porcelain manufactured in Germany in the town of that name. The technique used in painting the porcelain is normally the application of bright pure colours forming a myriad of stylised fantasy flowers on the white porcelain background. Dresden is best painted on hard paste fancy white porcelain without flaws and with a smooth glaze. Florets or flowers should suit the blank. Paint with a fast drying medium in brilliant colours that will not fire out.

Dresden thick oil   A pure prepared fat oil medium especially suited to European style painting.

Dry gold   Pure powdered gold.

Drying   Time is taken to allow paints or enamels to dry prior to the next step. Weather may play an important role in the length of drying time as does the medium used to mix paints and apply them.
Enamel Some enamels require several days drying time before firing otherwise they will chip off at a later date.
Dusting A fast drying medium usually requires a day or so to dry sufficiently in normal circumstances. Damp or cold weather will prolong the drying time.
Fat oil Layers of paint may be applied one on top of the other if

using this medium, provided they are allowed to dry between applications.

Dunting   Crazing of the glaze, usually caused by removing from the kiln while still hot or by gusts of cold air cooling the glaze too rapidly. Often done deliberately.

Dust   Natural enemy of all porcelain painters. Palettes and work should be kept covered and clean at all times.

Dusting   A method of applying dry powder paint to the surface of the porcelain. The usual method for dry dusting a painting is to paint your design normally, using a fast drying medium, then allow the painted object to become 'touch dry', that is you can touch the paint and feel it dry but with a very slight pull or tack. Using the dry powder colours that you originally painted with, sieved or squashed between greaseproof paper with the handle of your palette knife, and a ball of cotton wool, start with the lightest colours first and gently deposit the powder over areas of the same colour. When you have powder on all the areas you want to dust, rub the colour into the painted surface, once again starting with the lightest colour first and blending all the colours at the edges so that you do not end up with little circles of separate colour. Brush off excess powder and fire. The end result should be a pretty painting with softly blended colours and a high sheen. For an area of solid colour a little softer than a grounded area, the same method may be used. A word of caution. Wet looking areas will not dust well and after firing the paint may well blister and crack. It would be better to start again.

Earthenware   Coarse porous clay, fired low and therefore soft bodied. Glazed with lead or, as in the case of Delft or Faience, tin.

Eggs   Decorated eggs are popular. They come in glazed china or bisque or it is possible to paint on real eggs once emptied of their contents. Simply pierce both ends of the eggs and blow through one hole to force the contents through the other. Allow to dry and paint with normal porcelain paints and techniques. Spray with art varnish or fixative. A basket of painted eggs makes an inexpensive and delightful gift for Easter.

Embossed   Raised impression produced by stamping or the application of enamels or textures.

Emery paper   Fine emery paper or wet and dry sanding paper is used to rub painted pieces lightly to smooth the surface after firing, as particles of kiln dust will have adhered to the cooling glaze. There are several commercial preparations available from porcelain suppliers for this purpose as well and the humble Scotchbrite pot scourer may also be used.

Enamel A shiny, semi-transparent substance applied to porcelain to give a raised or textured design in relief. May be obtained in powder form and mixed with special enamel medium, your normal painting medium or a number of other products such as water based mediums, glycerine, grounding oil, Copaiba or turpentine for varied consistency and effects. It may also be purchased in a pre-mixed state. Enamel powder is more versatile than pre-mixed enamel and more tolerant of successive firings. Fired normally between 780–820° but as low as possible for continuous firings. Some white enamels may be coloured with a small amount of dry powder paint, $1/8$ to $1/6$ of the enamel powder used. This coloured enamel may be darker after firing as the white powder becomes transparent when matured in the kiln. Darker colours become a little lighter after firing. Care should be taken as many brands will chip off if not allowed to dry completely prior to firing. Enamels may be thinned with turps or a small amount may be left in the open air to thicken. Once fired, enamel may be painted or lustred and such additives as coloured glass fragments, shards, beach sand, semi precious gems or stones (some of which, like amethyst, lose their colour at normal firing temperatures) may be included. Most modern enamels will stand several fires and some may be fired as soon as applied. Always test fire a new enamel to see how it reacts to added colour and firing in your kiln. Enamel may shrink a little in the initial firing.

Enamel colours Metallic oxides, usually copper, iron and manganese, blended with powdered glass, for the decoration of metal, glass, porcelain and china.

English bone china Made from a soft bodied clay with a comparatively low fired glaze. Should not be fired above 820°C.

Engobe A coloured slip applied to clay bodies and fired high.

Environmentally-friendly burnish gold preparations do not contain mercury.

Eraser pencil There are several types of eraser pencils available. Soft tipped, firm, broad and narrow. Their uses are innumerable. What did we ever do without them? Use to draw in the wet paint, for sharp clear outlines and wipeouts, to apply pastes and enamels and so on.

Essence grasse Thickened turpentine or fat oil.

Etchall cream Commercial preparation of acid in cream form for etching glass and china. No longer readily available.

Etched Look Product which, when applied to glass, has the appearance of etching. There is also a *Matt Etched Look*. See Josephine's products.

Etching Matting the surface of the glazed porcelain by eating into it with acid.
Caution: Etching with hydrofluoric acid. Sketch a design the size of

the required etching and transfer it by tracing with the aid of graphite paper onto the porcelain. Using asphaltum paint the area *not to be etched*, completely covering the porcelain to protect it from the acid. Take care to see that the asphaltum is thick enough, and that there are no holes or brown areas. Cover all the porcelain not to be etched including the back or base of the piece. The asphaltum may have to be thinned from time to time to keep it flowing. Allow to dry a day or so and then place the object into an acid bath of 50% hydrofluoric acid for 1–2 minutes or until the etching is deep enough. Remove, and wash under running water to neutralise the acid. Wash with kerosene and then with hot soapy water to remove all traces of asphaltum and fire to further clean the porcelain. Please read more detailed instructions for etching than these if you wish to etch with acid. (*Porcelain Art in Australia Today*)

To etch with etching cream. Proceed as above until asphaltum has completely dried and then apply etching cream thickly over the areas to be etched. Leave for 12 to 24 hours, testing occasionally the depth of the etch. Clean as above. Although Etchall Cream is a commercial preparation no longer available, similar preparations should be treated with *extreme caution* as burns will result from the cream just as from the solution.

If acid comes into contact with your skin wash immediately in soda, soap and water to neutralise the acid. If severe, seek medical attention.

Eucalyptus oil   Fast drying light oil which is difficult to use but which allows crisp wipeouts.

European style   Traditional designs and techniques of the European porcelain factories.

Expressionism   Movement in art seeking to express emotional experience and reactions to reality.

Extruding   Shaping clay by passing it through a hollow lumen and forcing it out at the other end through a shaped opening.

Facilitator   A thinner to use Liquid Bright or Roman Gold.

Faience   Tin glazed pottery from central Europe.

Fat oil   Turpentine which has been evaporated and thickened and is used for mixing paints. The pigment is placed on a mixing tile or glass slab and mixed with oil of turpentine until a thick liquid is obtained. A drop or two of fat oil is then added and thoroughly mixed in.

Fauvism   Art movement typified by wild colours and emotional forms. A form of expressionism.

Faux-marbre   Marbelising.

Feather   1. To gently blend the wet paint on the object being painted with a broad square shader.

2. The outer covering of a bird.

Felspar   Group of minerals, such as potassium, aluminium, silicate, usually white in colour, occurring in crystals and granite, which is used in the making of porcelain, ceramics and enamels. *See* kaolin.

Ferrule   The metal grip which holds the hairs or bristles to a brush. The following information is courtesy of Alexander's:

There are differences in the ferrules used in the production of brushes. Alexander's consider that nickel plated brass ferrules are the best and most suitable for the uses to which porcelain painters put their brushes. The various types of ferrules are listed below in descending order of value:

1. Nickel plated brass *seamless*
2. Nickel plated soldered
3. Clear anodised aluminium seamless
4. Aluminium seamless, not anodised
5. Soldered tin
6. Unsoldered tin

A painter's hands would soon turn black using an aluminium ferrule. The term 'silver' may imply that it is a cheaper ferrule and not a nickel plated brass ferrule. Therefore the description of a brush which reads 'Sable hair, silver ferrule' would suggest a cheaper brush using inexpensive (so called) 'sable' hair with a nickel plated soldered ferrule.

Fibreglass brush   Used to burnish gold. Made up of lengths of glass or fibreglass fibres tied together with a cord which is gradually undone as the glass fibres become worn. Care must be taken to use the brush away from the painting area as minute particles of glass can contaminate the paints in the palette or fall on porcelain waiting to be fired, causing scarring as the glass melts in the kiln. The fibres also penetrate skin and cause irritation. Wear cotton clothing so that the fibres will not adhere as easily.

Filter   To carefully blend the applied paint while still wet with a square shader, so obtaining a soft finish with no distinct divisions of colour.

Findings   The settings for jewellery pieces.

Finger   A very useful tool. Wrapped in a small square of silk it will 'wipe out', blend, pad or lighten. Wrapped in a tissue or rubber surgical glove it will clean, define edges, and make strong stems or shapes and outlines. Discover its uses!

Firing The process of applying heat to a clay body for the purpose of vitrification or to allow the glaze to accept further decoration. Porcelain, china, glass etc is fired at sufficient heat to melt or soften the glaze so that it will absorb the paint pigments. The paint should be absorbed deeply enough to allow the glaze to be even and shining. Metallic paints do not sink into the glaze; they remain on the surface. Oils and impurities such as grease pencil marks, graphite etc burn off in the kiln during the firing. Some ball point pens do not fire out at comparatively low heats. The lowest part of the kiln is usually the coolest; however, individual kilns have different 'hot spots'. These are usually known or soon discovered by the owner. Most porcelain requires a range of 720°C to 900°C and the temperature elected should suit both the chinaware to be painted and the paints which are to be used. There should be a free flow of air in and around a stacked kiln during firing. Air vents should be open initially to allow fumes to escape when burning off. Glazed surfaces should not touch one another. If fired too hot, the colours will fade and sink deeply into the glaze, the glazed surface may craze, blister and roughen, particularly with soft glazes like some of the English and Belleek china. Some pinks will turn purple and some greens will turn brown. Yellow tends to become more intense and reds and oranges fade or become a dirty colour. If not fired high enough the glaze will be uneven with some matt areas and some colours, such as blue, will rub off. The first fire should be hot enough to attain a good even glossy glaze. Colour may be added later and, if you realise that as you apply colour you are also adding more flux, you will be aware that you will not need as high a temperature for subsequent firings. It is possible to fire fast without damage; however a slow fire is safer and surer, particularly with large pieces and tiles. The normal procedure recommended by the kiln manufacturing firm Tetlow is to switch on the kiln at a low setting for an hour to evaporate any water or dampness, leaving the vent open to allow the steam to escape. Then switch the kiln to a medium setting of 50 to 70 on the energy regulator and leave for another hour with the vent in position before switching to the highest setting. The vent should now stay closed until firing is complete. At this stage gas bubbles may escape through the glaze layer leaving craters and if firing is rapid there may not be enough time for these craters to be repaired in the softened glaze before the kiln is switched off. Once the kiln is switched off most of us leave it to do its own thing, however, another word of advice from Tetlow's. This information mainly applies to the initial application of glaze to the clay body but could affect later applications of paint as well. If the kiln takes too long to cool down to 750°C, the glossy surface may be dull. Alternatively matt glazes require a comparatively slow cooling period. Cooling may be accelerated by the partial or complete removal of the vent plug which should then be replaced for the later stages of the cooling process. The kiln should be allowed to cool slowly until the temperature drops to approximately 130°C, when the process can then be speeded up again by the removal of the vent plug and the progressive opening of the door. There is kiln furniture available to stack a kiln. It is safest to stack plates, plaques and tiles on their edges. (The only accidents I have had have been with plates stacked on tripods or stilts. Never again!) Do not stack tiles against elements as the uneven heat may cause breakage, and do not cram or wedge pieces in as there is need for expansion. If plates are stacked one on top of the other the weight may cause breakage and the stilts may penetrate the glaze. Glazed surfaces should not touch although the unglazed surfaces and rims may do so.

The manufacturer's instructions should be followed, but a general rule of thumb would be to fire your kiln for half an hour or so on low, with the vent open to allow fumes to escape, a further 30 minutes on medium and then high until the desired temperature is reached. For large tiles or a partially filled kiln, slow the rate of firing if necessary. To fire glass, place it on the floor of the kiln with space all around.

Firing tree   Kiln furniture designed to hold ornaments, beads and eggs etc. Will not fire high but suitable for porcelain temperatures. Made of nichrome wire and obtainable from ceramic stockists.

Fit   A glaze should fit or completely cover the entire body of a clay object.

Flairs   Trade name for glass particles used for decoration. Fired at Cone 22 or 600°C. Balsam of copaiba or mineral oil is brushed onto the otherwise completed piece and the flairs or frosts are sprinkled on. Firing at a higher temperature may cause the particles to pop off. *See* Frosts.

Flaking   As for glass excising.

Flat enamel painting   The application of flat enamel similar to the enamel paintings of the Limoges factory. The difference between enamels and porcelain paints is that enamels are opaque, have body and sit on the glaze as relief work whereas porcelain paints are flat (or should be), transparent and are embedded in the glaze during firing. Try it on a tile first as it is important that your enamel expands and contracts with the porcelain. First tint your piece with the colour that is to be left on any exposed porcelain. Fire and pen in your black (mixed with a little of another colour to soften it) or gold outlines. Fire again. Mix your enamel with fat oil or Dresden thick oil (I have used Base for Raised Gold with a Copaiba based medium) until a thick paste, add a little flux powder and thin with lavender oil to almost liquid, with enough body to flatten and smooth itself out without running all over the place. Apply with a soft brush smoothly and evenly, allowing for expansion to the penned lines. If it overlaps the line, quickly and carefully wipe back. The aim is to produce smooth and even areas of brilliant colour. Fire the enamel only once and as low as it will tolerate, to prevent chipping.

Flat tint   A wash of colour over the surface that does not vary in tone, depth or intensity.

Fleur-de-lis   An iris of conventional design used in heraldry.

Flint   Hard stone of almost pure silica.

Flint china   Hard dense earthenware, similar to ironware.

Floating   Spreading enamel or paste to cover an area such as a petal or leaf. The edges are usually left slightly raised.

Flow on enamel   To flood enamel onto a porcelain surface.

Flux   Substance composed of borax, soda, lead and sand, used to facilitate fusion. The pigments in powder paints are all mineral, fuse at different temperatures and require the additon of flux to help them melt at a uniform temperature. Colours with too much flux appear transparent and cloudy. Some colours such as blues work better with the addition of a little flux to the dry powder prior to grinding with oil. Colours which have been fluxed will mature at a lower temperature and have a high glaze. Crystal Clear is a clear powder paint consisting of a great deal of flux which may be used for dusting an object which has been painted and fired and which will give it a high gloss, however, too much flux will destroy or 'eat' some colours and it is difficult to replace them because of the amount of flux in the glaze. Gold may be purchased both fluxed and unfluxed. Unfluxed gold is for use over painted areas where the paint already contains flux.

Focal point   The area which should dominate the painting. It may be a single feature or a group of objects placed in a well balanced position in the design, usually one third in, one third up or one third down. *See* diagram on next page.

Foot   The base of a vase or urn.

Foreground   That part of the design which is closest to the viewer. Detail is clear, sharp and 'in focus'. There is no clear dividing line between fore and middle ground. One area blends gently into the other.

Foreshortening   Exaggerated perspective applied to single objects or figures.

Form   The external shape or appearance of an object.

Formula 10   An odourless all purpose open medium suitable for mixing, painting and brush conditioning, which allows for heavy

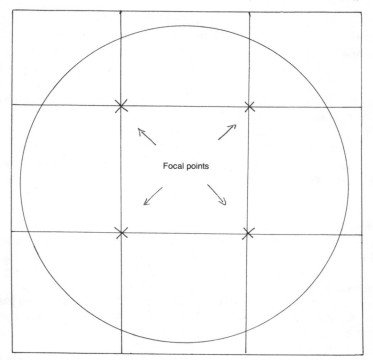

Focal points

application in one fire work or light appliction for washes.

Found line Obvious separation in design, such as the edge of light against dark objects, eg dark ball on white paper. Opposite to a lost line, where values and colours are similar and the division is difficult to see.

Frame Construction to surround and hold in place a painting.

Free hand To make a drawing of a subject without sketching aids.

Fresco The method of painting with powdered pigments mixed with water and applying to plaster walls or ceiling before the plaster is dry.

Fret Carved or embossed work in decorative patterns, often interlaced or intersecting repetitive designs.

Frieze Decorated band, usually around walls.

Frit 1. A recipe for glazes using such glazing materials as flint or silica sand that has already been fired and ground finely for use as low and medium fire glazes.
2. Soluble or toxic materials are melted together with insoluble materials, cooled rapidly, fractured in cold water and powdered to render highly toxic materials less toxic.

Frosts   Trade name for glass particles. As for Flairs.

Frottis   A French term used for a wash of colour or glaze.

Fugitive colours   Colours in which the pigments react to those in other colours or to the heat of the kiln. Yellows and reds are a good example.

Full brush   The hairs of the brush are loaded with oil so that it acts as a 'tank' to carry the paint.

Full load   A fully loaded brush is an oil filled brush loaded with paint right across its width.

Furniture   For the kiln. The shelves, shelf props, tile and plate racks and stilts etc which are used in the process of firing.

Gild   To paint with gold.

Glass   Non-crystalline solid substance, usually transparent, which provides us with a similar surface to porcelain on which to paint. There are especially manufactured glass paints which mature at a lower temperature more suited to glass objects and the same techniques are used to apply the paint. Extreme care is needed to blend the paint and eliminate brush strokes as, when lit from within or behind, every brushstroke, speck of dust and paint build-up seems to take on enormous and obvious dimensions.

To paint inexpensive glass. Before buying an expensive glass lamp try painting on a cheaper piece. You may use your low firing china paints or add flux, however you will probably achieve better results if you use glass paints. Use a fast drying medium, not an open medium or a mineral oil. Glass objects will tolerate repeated firings if fired correctly. Mix your paints with the medium and give the object you are painting a wash of pastel colour. Fire at 600°C. It is a good idea to paint a kiln wash over the shelves of the kiln to protect them. Place the painted objects well apart on a shelf about the lower middle of the kiln. Fire slowly for the first hour with the kiln ventilated, then gradually bring the temperature to maturity. Allow to cool in its own time. Paint with your design and repeat firing process.

Used as decoration and to remove glaze. For decorative purposes pieces of glass, clear or coloured glass beads are adhered to the porcelain with the aid of flux mixed with a medium (almost any will do) and fired at a suitable temperature. There are so many types of glass that it is difficult to state a particular temperature. As a general rule glass pieces fired under 800°C will retain their original shape, whereas over 800°C they tend to become smooth and rounded. A subsequent fire to colour it should be as low as possible as the glass may chip off with further firings. Pieces of coloured glass or beads may be embedded in the texture pastes and coloured with a lustre on the upper surface of the glass in the final fire. The threading holes in glass beads may be filled with smaller beads. Because of all the factors involved in firing glass, ie the type, thickness, size, position, the various mediums which can be used to adhere it to the porcelain, the drying time, the length of time individual kilns take to reach a temperature, actual temperature, cooling time and the human element, it is impossible to accurately forecast the results.

Glass beads   As for glass sand. Available from porcelain suppliers.

Glass chipping   As for glass excising.

Glass excising   Removing the glaze from the porcelain body with glass sand or excising beads. 'Resist' that part of the porcelain which is not to be excised and paint the area from which the glaze is to be removed with a mixture of flux ground with medium to a liquid, keeping away from plate and vase rims. Excising close to the rims of objects may leave a sharp edge. Pour the glass sand or excising beads onto the wet area and press as many as possible into the flux mixture, using as much glass as the mix will absorb. Clean rims and remove masking lacquer and any beads of glass on clear part of porcelain. Fire high. As it cools the glass will contract at a faster rate than the glaze on the porcelain body and should be able to be flaked off easily or with the aid of a sharp flat tool. Take care with flying glass chips and wear protective glasses or goggles, heavy gloves and protective clothing. If some of the glass is reluctant, simply refire until it eventually comes off. It may look interesting where it is, however it will eventually pop off with the natural contraction and expansion of the porcelain. Excising is a perfect way to disguise marred, chipped or badly painted porcelain. To make your own ground glass choose old bottles, soft glass which is not plasticised or hardened as this is difficult to remove.

Glass gold   A gold preparation for use on glass to be fired at comparatively lower temperatures.

Glass palette   Small square of heavy roughened glass on which to grind paints. It should not be used as a palette as the 'tooth' of the roughened glass will damage the hairs of a brush very quickly.

Glass sand   Fine particles of glass which may be applied to a glazed porcelain surface with the aid of medium and flux and fired to remove the glaze. Take care not to leave particles of glass on the parts of porcelain you want to remain smooth as they will leave marks on the surface. It is available in coarse, medium and fine particles and the resultant pattern left on the porcelain body depends on the size of the particles, type of porcelain, thickness of the application of glass sand or beads, heat of the kiln, length of the kiln cycle of firing time, amounts of medium and flux, and many other variables.

Glaze   Vitreous (glass-like) substance containing silica, white lead, ground glass and talc is fixed by fusion to the clay body or bisque to give it a smooth gloss surface.

Glue   To use glue as a pen oil, mix your powder paints with a couple of drops of mucilage and thin with water to running consistency. The mixture dries quickly and it is possible to use normal paints mixed with oil over the penwork.

Glycerine   May be used as a waterbased medium to mix paints and adhere the paint to the porcelain surface.

Gold chasing or patterned gold. To chase gold requires several fires. Firstly paint the design in gold and fire. Polish with a glass brush and wash well afterwards to remove any glass particles. Paint again with gold, fire and rub with burnishing sand for a brilliant finish. Outline the design, taking care not to mark the gold. Put in detail, such as veins on leaves, highlights and shading etc with fine penwork and fire again. The previously painted gold will have a beautiful finish and should be left. The latest application is then chased or rubbed with a pointed pencil shaped agate. Every line is polished, highlights rubbed, and veins of leaves and shading are polished to accentuate the design and emphasize the linear separations. The whole design is then softened with a fine glass burnishing brush.

Gold colours   Colours which contain gold, usually the roses, rubies and purples which are fired high in order to mature them.

Gold eraser   Hard substance used primarily for removing the purple smudges and finger marks left by careless cleaning. However, will remove gold and lustres if the rubber is applied diligently.

Gold printing   Pressing an object such as a leaf which has been coated with gold onto a mother of pearl or plain white porcelain surface.

Gouache   Matt colours.

Graphite outline   Trace your design with graphite paper and dust the outline with powdered paint the colour of your choice. For a pale outline, dust a much lighter colour. Fire.

Graphite paper   A type of carbon paper used for tracing.

Graphite pencil   A pencil capable of writing on china. The lines drawn will burn off when fired.

Grease pencil   Used to draw and write on porcelain. Will fire off in kiln. It could act as a resist to applied colours, lustres and metallics.

Greenware   Raw porcelain clay not yet fired.

Grey scale   The scale of values.

Greyed colour   Another colour is added to lower the intensity of a hue. A primary colour may be greyed to paint some area of the background so that the general tone of the design is repeated throughout.

Grind To grind the powdered paint pigments to a toothpaste or thick cream consistency, start by tapping the base of phial of powder on a flat surface to settle the contents and avoid spillage when the lid is removed. The fine powder, if spilled, could land anywhere, on the surface you are painting, in your palette or on the work of the person sitting next to you. Place some powder onto a tile or ground glass slab and with your cleaned palette knife remove some grinding oil from its container and place it on the slab as well but away from the powder. The oil you use to grind the paints may be a commercially prepared grinding oil or one of the open or slow drying mediums, paraffin oil or other oil of your choice, which will keep your paints workable for several weeks or longer but they will have collected a lot of dust by then. Alternatively, you may use a copaiba based medium which produces a less slippery result than the open oils; however your paints will harden in just a few days. Take some of the oil with the palette knife and, using a circular motion and the flat surface of the knife, mix oil and paint powder together. Take more oil if necessary but do not add it all at once as it may be too much and you will then have to add more powder. Continue mixing until it is well mixed and there are no grainy particles left. Some colours require much more mixing than others because of their gritty nature and may well be helped by first grinding with a little methylated spirits.

Grisaille Monochrome in shades of grey to resemble a relief sculpture.

Grounding Application of a rich solid area of colour to an area, usually a border, of a piece of porcelain. The porcelain is cleaned well and the area *not* to be grounded is protected with a masking lacquer. Mix a little of the powder paint you intend to use with grounding oil and paint the area to be grounded. The small amount of colour in the oil will let you see where you have been. Make sure that the entire area is covered as it is very difficult to repair. Allow the grounding oil to dry for a few minutes and then pad with a silk pad to smooth and even out the oil. The area will be ready to apply the powder paint when the oil feels tacky on the silk pad and makes a sticking sound when padded. There is a slight pull on the pad. Place dry powder in a piece of stocking or place a piece of stocking over the top of the paint phial and fix in place with an elastic band. Sprinkle the powder liberally over the oiled area without touching the surface and covering it entirely. Using a large dusting brush, gently press the powder into the oil and, with a circular motion, work in as much of the powder as the oil will absorb without touching the oily surface with the brush. It should look dry and matt. When you are sure it will take no more powder and has an even matt appearance, brush the superfluous powder off and leave awhile. Check later to see that no damp patches have appeared and, if they have, reapply more powder to these areas.

However, if these damp areas are too oily, the wise thing to do would be to take it all off and start again as too much oil will absorb too much powder and the result will be chipping and crazing. Remove the masking lacquer and clean any powder from the rest of the object, including the back, the base and inside, using methylated spirits as this will not run into the powder as mineral turpentine does. An interesting effect may be obtained by grounding a surface, allowing to dry, and, with a selection of sharp pointed tools, both thick and thin, scratching out a 'penwork' design. This is easier if the grounding is fired to approximately 400°C before scratching.

Grounding oil   A heavy fast drying oil used for grounding.

Gum arabic   May be added to enamel if for allergy reasons the enamel is mixed with water.

Half-fired   A surface may be painted with a solid colour, fired to approximately 400°C and removed from the kiln. The paint is dry enough to touch without marring it and a design may be drawn onto it, scratched into it or paint removed from it in a pattern. The firing process is recommenced and the design fired in. It is possible to obtain a very precise and intricate pattern in this way.

Half tone   Area leading away from light source.

Halo effect   When part of the design is completely encircled by a single background colour. To avoid this, first select three areas where you can 'cut in' with a dark colour for depth, usually a division of petals, next load your brush with a medium to light shade and place some background against the dark portions of the design, then medium to dark colours for placement next to the lighter areas. Next load your brush with colours which will 'reflect' other parts of your design. This should give you a variety of background colours which will blend together to show depth under the area, contrast and draw in the rest of the design for support. Always use each colour in your design more than once otherwise that colour will look very lonely. And a rainbow effect is almost as bad as a halo effect. (You can't win, can you?) Keep your applications of colour varied in size and shape and avoid repeating the order in which you apply colours.

Hancock's raised paste   Yellow powder for raised paste under gold.

Hancock's raised paste medium   Medium for mixing Hancock's raised paste.

Handrest   A simple handrest is built by attaching two corks or small blocks of wood to the underside of each end of a flat ruler. *See* p. 53.

Tawny Frogmouths
1st and 2nd fire

3rd fire
(Photography A. Patten)

Roses
Background, applied at random leaving light and
options

Roses
1st fire—
shapes of
flowers
identified in
background
and 'wiped
out'.

2nd fire

3rd fire

Handrest

Hanovia Cerama-pen Liquid Bright Gold pen for penwork or decoration. To start, remove cap and depress tip on piece of paper. Hold until gold appears on tip. Write slowly and evenly to allow for adequate flow of gold. If tip wears down before gold is depleted, replace it by inserting the spare tip stored in the top of the pen. Recap tightly to prevent possible evaporation. Fire as you would for ordinary Liquid Bright Gold.

Hanovia gold and lustres Brand of gold and lustres.

Hard glaze porcelain Japanese, German and French porcelain are considered hard glaze porcelain bodies and are capable of taking a high fire (860°C).

Hard paste Refers to true porcelain clay body.

Harmonious colour Colour combinations of several hues which have a good relationship. There are names given to the most commonly used combinations. *See* diagram on page 54.

Health hazards There are a number of health hazards for the porcelain artist to know about. Firstly the *paints*. Paints are composed of oxides and salts of elements and they must be fired at a temperature sufficiently hot to mature them, which in turn requires the use of a flux to react with and assist in dissolving all the particles. One example of a flux is *lead oxide*. The other elements with which we paint, besides lead, may be *cadmium, cobalt, copper, gold, iron, manganese, silica* and *zinc*. These could be dangerous if inhaled or taken into the mouth in quantity. Precautions to be taken should include the wearing of a suitable mask when decanting powdered colours, dusting or grounding. Do not shape your brush by putting it in your mouth. Do not prepare, eat food or smoke with hands on which there is still paint. Note the lead content of paints and try to avoid using paint with a high lead content on food utensils. Fire paints which contain lead at the correct temperature. Secondly, the *acids*. An acid burn is horrific. It is not merely superficial

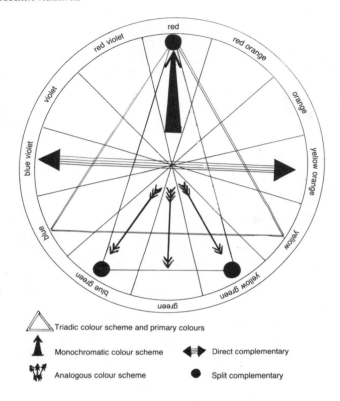

Harmonious colours

but continues to penetrate the tissues deeply even after the surface is neutralised. *Caution with acids.* Wash with soap and water, baking soda and seek medical attention if the burn is extensive.

Glass excising. This can be dangerous if precautions are not taken. Wear protective glasses and gloves when chipping the glass from the body of the porcelain.

Allergies: a matter for the individual. Avoid using the products to which you are allergic. There is bound to be an alternative.

Because of the complete involvement the porcelain painter has with the art there are compensations for the health hazards in the form of therapeutic value. Most painters seem to have the ability to shut out the rest of the world, with all its material cares and worries, while they are painting. Loneliness becomes a thing of the past and the main need for company is the desire to paint with others in order to share and benefit from the combined stimulation and ideas generated in a group situation. The only hazard caused by this is lack of understanding from the rest of the immediate family.

Heavy oil   Fast drying oil such as oil of copaiba.

Highlight   That part of the design which is the focal point of the light. The area closest to the light.

History of origins of porcelain   The use of clay as a utility vehicle for cooking and water originated in very early times. Ancient historical and archeological discoveries have proved that the Egyptians used glass as a glaze as early as the Fourth Dynasty and tin glazes were used for wall tile pictures as early as 500 BC. Metallic oxides were used for decoration by other races of that era. Turquoise blue was derived from copper by the Assyrians and Babylonians. Civilization was mainly concentrated around the eastern Mediterranean area and technology developed in one country soon found its way to another, with minor changes in the decoration.

Porcelain is distinct from pottery in that it is translucent and, when broken, displays a clean smooth fracture. Pottery is opaque and the break is rough. The name is derived from the Chinese terms 'kaolin' and 'petuntse' and is known as 'hard paste'. Artificial porcelain is known as 'soft paste'.

Hard paste contains only the natural elements of china clay and feldspar, whereas soft paste porcelain is made up of combinations of clays, animal and mineral ingredients. The terms 'hard' and 'soft' refer to the degree of firing required by the clay bodies to vitrify them.

Pieces of porcelain from China first appeared in Britain in 1506, although there are stories of earlier pieces being brought across land from the Orient. It was not until the early 1700s that the secret of porcelain manufacture reached Paris and Sevres. Porcelain factories were able to commence production in Europe and porcelain began to replace tin glazed pottery from Majolica and other popular ceramic factories.

There are pieces of porcelain which date back prior to that date from Italy, such as the Medici porcelain and porcelain from Venice, but these were not produced in commercial quantity and the secret of their production was very well kept. The first true hard paste porcelain was produced in Europe in Saxony in 1709 and in 1709 the Meissen factory commenced production under the direction of Bottger. In England factories commenced production around 1745 with Worcester, Bow, Derby, Rockingham and several others all being founded in the next ten years.

Hogarth curve   Line of design in the shape of an elongated 'S'.

Horizon   A horizon line is needed in most paintings and designs even if it has to be imagined. It should never be in the centre to 'cut the design in half', but a little to the top of or below the centre.

Horn knife   Horn or bone palette knives are useful for mixing gold and other metallics. Not readily available now but easily made from the handles of old cutlery for the purist painter.

Hue   Name given to a colour.

Hybrid hard paste porcelain   Hard paste porcelain with the addition of magnesite and quartz.

Hydrofluoric acid   *Caution.* Very dangerous acid which should be used with extreme care to etch china. This acid will continue to eat into your tissues should it come in contact with them. For those people conscious of damage which may be done to the ozone layer by the use of chlorofluorocarbons, it is not impossible to produce these light substances from the heavy hydrofluoric and hydrochloric acids through the actions of etching and leaching as described in this book.

Icon   Originally conventional paintings of Christ and the Saints of Grecian design. Now used for any image in art.

Illusionism   The art of extending an indoor scene into the outdoor area with the use of painted windows or doors and scenes beyond, taking advantage of perspective and foreshortening, light and colour.

Imari   Japanese ware, usually with geometric design.

Impasto   Raised decoration in enamel or slip on ceramics.

Impressionism   Method of painting ascribed to French artists who painted the momentary or transitory appearance of things, particularly the effects of light and atmosphere as opposed to form or structure.

Impressionistic   Not an exact reproduction of the subject but rather an artist's impression.

Incising paste   A commercially prepared paste which is applied to the porcelain and covered with a specific type of glass or incising beads. During the firing process the glass fuses with the paste and glaze causing the glaze to crack and chip off when, during the cooling process, the glass contracts at a faster rate than the glaze, to expose the body or bisque of the clay. Because of the variables involved, ie the amount of paste, type and size of the grains of glass, glaze and body of the object, length of firing time and temperature, it is impossible to predict the resulting pattern. The exposed clay body may be painted with lustres, Liquid Bright Gold or metallic paints.

Indian ink   A design may be drawn in Indian ink, painted over without being moved, and the ink will disappear in the firing process.

Ink   Thin fluid used for penwork or writing text. May be made up with pen oil and powder paint to ink consistency. A quick alternative is to add a little turpentine to mixed paint from your palette.

Inspiration   The stimulating ideas we all have from time to time.

Intensify   To strengthen colour with further applications or to strengthen a design with contrasting depth or detail.

Intensity   Brightness of colour value.

Interpretation   Each artist puts his or her own interpretation or ideas of a subject into the design.

I-Relief   Substance introduced from Denmark to add structure to the porcelain form. It is a ceramic composition which may be used on porcelain, china and tiles and on the body of the porcelain once the glaze has been removed. It can be mixed with a variety of solutions, mediums, water-based mediums, simple syrups, milk etc. Almost anything to bring it to a thick cream consistency. It should be thick enough to hold its shape and may be applied with a stylus, brush, sponge, anything to obtain the effect you want. Such additives as powdered paints (in small quantities, ie ⅛), enamel paints of the copper enamelling variety, sand, glass fragments etc may be included in the mix. After firing it may be coloured with Liquid Bright Gold, lustres, paints etc. It will fire at a wide range of temperatures, being more glossy and rounded with higher temperatures, while holding its shape and having a semi-matt finish at lower temperatures. As with most structural substances it will not tolerate successive hot firings happily and should only be fired at the lowest temperature suited to mature the lustre, gold or paint requiring the further firing.

Iron colours   Red colours containing iron oxide whch are usually fired at a low temperature ie 720–760°C. Iron colours do not mix well with yellows, although some recent colours have been developed which are more adaptable.

Ironstone   Hard dense earthenware from Staffordshire, similar to Spode stone china.

Ivory vellum   Cream coloured powder which, when dusted onto porcelain and fired, will give a creamy matt surface similar to bisque finish. May then be painted with matt colours.

Japanese bone china   A clay body made up with approximately ⅓ calcined bone or bone ash. It is able to take a higher firing than English bone china which has a higher content of bone ash.

Jewelling   Enamel applied to look like jewels. It is either coloured before application or painted afterwards.

Judging   When your work is judged professionally, the judge looks for the following: Originality, composition and colour harmony, proportion, technique, finish, firing and attention to detail. The initial impact or first impression is of utmost importance and the viewer frequently does not know why he or she likes or dislikes a painting. Art is very much a matter of personal opinion, however it is the judge's opinion and the value placed on the judging points which count in this case. Usually the judge awards a point score for each of the artistic requirements such as 6, 7 or 8 out of 10 and then totals the result which provides a fair and accurate grading.

Originality The work should be the original work of the artist. Copies of even the Great Masters will lose marks for lack of originality.

Composition and colour harmony The composition or design should be balanced and the viewer's eye should go immediately to the focal point or centre of interest. The lines of the design should then lead the gaze around the supporting features and not off the painting. There should be a balance between painted design and negative space and the groups of design should also balance in size (that does not mean they should be the same size) and relate to each other in position and the way they connect with one another.

Colour harmony is a colour combination that does not glare and fight with itself. The colour scheme should be pleasing to the eye, well balanced and have a variety of values to give the painting a third dimension.

Proportion Relative size of subject matter.

Technique Suitability of application of design, quality of brushwork, penwork, additives such as enamelling, glass, gold and grounding etc.

Finish Attention to detail, cleanliness and presentation. In fact, presentation is often half the battle.

Firing A smooth evenly glazed surface with no 'flat' spots or chipped or crazed surface is the desired appearance.

Kakiemon   Asymmetrical designs from Japan.

Kaolin   China clay used in making porcelain, formed by decomposition and weathering of feldspar in granite.

Kemper pen   For fine line drawing with liquid gold solutions. The pen consists of a handle with a small tank that has a funnel-shaped outlet. The tank is filled with gold liquid and used with a normal writing motion. Must be kept clean at all times.

Kiln   Furnace for drying and maturing paints on your porcelain. Not all kilns are calibrated to the temperatures they read and should be tested for accuracy occasionally with cones if you do not already use cones to fire. Most kilns in Australia are electric and to work out the cost of firing your kiln multiply the amps by the voltage which will give the number of watts used and multiply this sum by the current cost of a kilowatt hour and adjust by the number of hours it takes to fire your kiln. There are a number available and it is a matter of personal taste and finance when you make your choice. The most common is an electric kiln with an inner chamber measuring 32.5 x 32.5 x 32.5 cm (13 x 13 x 13 inches) with built in temperature control and which automatically turns off when the desired temperature is reached. These kilns are 240 volts, 10 amps and 1 phase which plug into any household power outlet. (15 amp kilns should be professionally installed). These kilns are fitted with an energy regulator to control the rate of temperature rise, a warning light, safety switch which turns the kiln off should you open the door, a spy hole in the door, and a vent in the roof. However, it is possible to obtain smaller kilns, larger kilns, round kilns, gas kilns, kilns which are not automatic and custom built kilns with digital readouts.

The following information was provided by the various manufacturers and in places has been condensed, however more complete information would be available on application from the firms or from your retailer.

Ceramic kiln makers 38 Longerenong St. Farrer ACT 2607. All kiln casings are of welded aluminium construction with a ceramic fibre lay-up which consists of 5 layers of 25 mm fibre. Four layers of 100 kg per cubic metre density, with the hot face layer 160 kg per cubic metre density. Stand and shelf, and an optional extra is a fully programmable microprocessor. 2.4 KW, 240 volt, single phase, AC supply. 2 m power lead, 3 pin plug. There are regular sizes, however kilns can be constructed to suit individual requirements.

Cromartie Kilns Ltd Prior Industries NSW Pty Ltd PO Box 918 Bankstown NSW 2200 and PO Box 276 Acacia Ridge Queensland 4110. Top loading kilns available in various sizes and both round and oval with an approved interlocking lid safety switch, lockable lid catch, adjustable lid stay, heat resistant handle, lockable castor wheels, easy to change elements, mains 'on' warning light, energy regulator/s, plug in control socket, choice of temperature control system, ventilation plug/s in lid. The construction is of a mirror finish stainless steel jacket surrounding a lining of 75 mm (3″) fuel efficient light weight bricks backed with a thick layer of ceramic fibre. The kiln load is supported by an all brick floor and the lid is lined with ceramic fibre. Capable of 1300°C. There is a range of temperature controls available such as a pyrometer which is either analogue or digital, kiln sitter with limit timer, electronic controllers ranging from a simple soak/cut-off feature to a highly sophisticated multi-ramp, mutli-dwell digital computer.

B. & L. Tetlow Pty Ltd 12 George Street, Blackburn Vic. 3130. An extensive range of kilns is available and Tetlow recommends that kilns used for porcelain be clad in stainless steel for maximum life expectancy. It is possible to get highly corrosive acid as a by-product during the normal firing process which may shorten the life of a mild steel kiln.

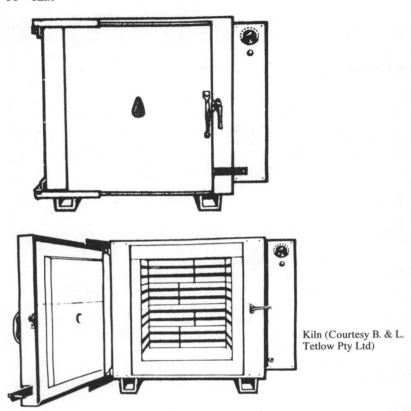

Kiln (Courtesy B. & L. Tetlow Pty Ltd)

There is a comprehensive manual available with the kilns which is most informative on all aspects of firing.

The bricks used for electric kilns are of the refractory insulation type. All kilns are fitted with an energy regulator complete with a pilot light which switches on and off automatically as the energy regulator switches the current to the elements on and off. The most common elements used are Kanthal A1 which are made from alloys of iron, aluminium chromium and cobalt and operate to a temperature of 1300°C. Before any kiln is put into use, it should be fired slowly, preferably over two or three days, to a temperature no higher than 100 or 200 degrees below the maximum firing temperature for which it is designed. This slow firing will remove any moisture from the brickwork.

Accessories

Energy Regulator Used to control rate of temperature increase. Controlled by a knob which is calibrated from 1–100%. If 50% is selected the electricity supply to the elements is stopped for half of a given time, eg on for 5 seconds and off for 5 seconds then on again for a further five seconds and so on.

Door switch A mechanical contact which interrupts the flow of electricity to the elements when the door is opened.

Time clock A timing device which allows one to pre-set the time at which the kiln is activated by setting one of the pointers to the commencing time and another pointer is set to the finishing time. Some clocks have day control as well as hour control.

Pyrometers and pyroscopes Pyrometers measure temperature and pyroscopes measure heat work. Pyroscopes are indicators made of ceramic mixtures based on silicates which bend when heated to a certain temperature.

Cones are commonly classified as pyroscopes and come in two sizes, *standard* (2½″ tall) and *miniature* (1″ tall). They are made of carefully controlled mixtures of ceramic materials designed to give a graduated scale of fusing temperatures at approximately 20 degree intervals. The cones will melt and collapse when they have been subjected to a certain temperature or rate of temperature increase for a length of time. That is to say a temperature attained rapidly will not have the same maturing effect as the same temperature reached slowly. It is important to mount the cones correctly and it is usual to use three cones for each firing, one about 20 degrees below the desired temperature, another indicating the temperature at which the ware is to be fired and the third about 20 degrees higher.

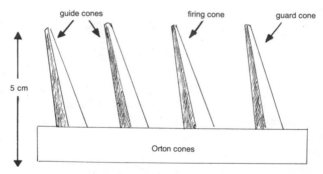

Kiln shelves or 'bats' Each bat should be supported at three points as this prevents rocking, which may occur if the bat was supported at each of its four corners. The supports should be placed in the same position for each shelf inserted so that the weight is distributed in a downward column. The shelves should be painted with a commercial kiln wash or one made of a mixture of alumina and china clay or zircon and china clay mixed with water. The shelves and props are usually made from sillimanite or a mixture of similar materials. For a bisque fire pots may touch, however allowance should be made for shrinkage. All clayware placed in the kiln must be dry as damp ware is likely to crack and may explode as a result of steam pressure built up inside it when firing begins. Ware placed in a kiln for a glost fire must not have glazed surfaces touching.

To fire Remove the vent plug and if desired the spy hole may be left open as well. Set the energy regulator at a fairly low setting to evaporate any surface moisture. After an hour increase the setting to about 50 to 70% and leave for a further hour. The vent plug should be in position during this period and should remain in position until firing finishes.

Kiln care   Vacuum your kiln occasionally. Dry your kiln before its initial use and after prolonged disuse by heating for a short time.

Kiln furniture   The shelves, posts, plate and tile stands and stilts used in firing.

Kiln sitter   An optional extra for your kiln which will turn it off once it has reached the desired temperature.

Kiln wash   A wash composed of dry powder and water and applied to kiln furniture and the floor of the kiln to protect the firebricks against dripping glazes and paints.

Lampblack   Black powder placed in a soft cloth and tied into a pad. A design is drawn onto tracing paper and pinprick perforations are made along its outline. The paper is attached to the piece to be painted and gently padded with the lampblack pad which allows the powder to penetrate the holes and reproduce the pattern.

Lavender oil   Oil used to keep medium open and usable for longer periods of time.

Laying in colour   Filling in the shape of the object being painted with a flat well loaded brush. It may or may not be outlined.

Leach   To draw out or purge part of a substance. Some lead is leached from paint during firing by the action of heat and some may be leached from glaze by fluids during domestic use.

Lead flower   Term given to main flower in design.

Lead glaze   A reliable low fired flux commonly used.

Lead in paints   Most colours have a certain amount of lead in them as it acts as a flux and manufacturers, these days, state on the label the lead content in percentage form. Liquids and especially liquids containing acids draw out the lead from the paint even after it has been fired and this is why it is not wise to use a paint with a heavy concentrate of lead on food or utility vessels. If the articles are fired at the correct temperature most of the lead will be leached out during the firing process. It is therefore important to follow the manufacturers' directions if a temperature range is suggested. When using paints, care should be taken not to transfer the paint from hand or brush to mouth, or with dry powder, not to inhale the particles of paint dust.

Leading lady   Term given to main flower in design.

Leatherhard   A clay body not yet fired, which can be further shaped and carved.

Legends   *Dogwood* The Dogwood used to be a huge strong tree and it was used for the cross on which Jesus was crucified. The tree was so upset at being used for this purpose that it decided it would never again be big and strong. Its blossoms are in the form of a cross, two long and two short petals. In the centre of the outer edge of each petal there are nail prints, brown with rust and stained with red. In the centre of the flower is a crown of thorns.

Rose One day Chloris was walking in the woods and came upon a dead nymph. She decided to turn her into a flower, but thought her too pretty to be an ordinary flower and asked the other gods for advice. Dionysius donated nectar, the Three Graces bestowed charm and elegance, Aphrodite, goddess of love and beauty, gave these as gifts. The result was so beautiful that they made the flower the Queen of Flowers and named it the Rose.

Pansy Once there was a woodsman who lived with his two daughters, and who married a widow who also had two daughters. He was worried because there were only five chairs. However the widow had ideas of her own and took command. She sat at the head of the table and because her skirts were so wide she sat on two chairs. She placed her daughters who were almost as well dressed and always in the same colours either side of her. The two plump daughters of the woodsman sat at the end of the table on the remaining chair. If you study the pansy you will see that the full skirted petal sits on two sepals, the two colourful petals next to it sit on a sepal each and the two large petals (daughters of the woodsman) share a sepal at the top of the flower. And the poor woodsman? Well, if you look under the flower you will see a trumpet shaped spur which is for water storage. This is the basement of the cottage and the woodsman sits down there with his feet in the water to keep warm.

Another pansy story to help paint these flowers. There was a lady who lived in a tent and who had two favourite daughters who were always by their mother's side and who always wore the same colour dress. There were also two fat twin stepsisters who always dressed alike. The tent is the inverted 'V' which is the first part of the pansy to be painted. It gives both position and direction. Next the mother in her full skirt with the two daughters, one either side in the same colour and finally the two large petals, often a different colour from the rest of the family or flower but always the same as each other.

Light   Without light we could not see. The artist must create the illusion of light in a painting. A *highlight* is where light from the light source falls directly on the subject.

Diffused light is softened and widespread.

Filtered light is patchy where obstructed by objects in its path.

Reflected light is light thrown off one object onto another and it will carry the colour of that object with it.

Transmitted light is light rays shining through an object.

Light source   Direction from which light falls on subject.

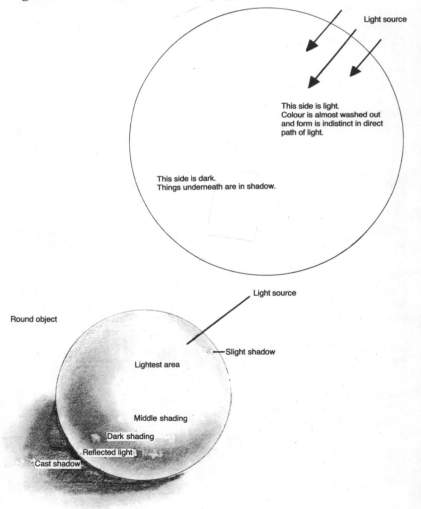

Light source

This side is light.
Colour is almost washed out
and form is indistinct in direct
path of light.

This side is dark.
Things underneath are in shadow.

Light source

Round object

Slight shadow

Lightest area

Middle shading

Dark shading

Reflected light

Cast shadow

Limit timer A device used to switch off a kiln at a desired temperature.

Limited palette A palette consisting of six or seven colours maximum for all your requirements.

Line The line of design is the path where all the action is. All lines have direction which the viewer's eye will follow. A line leading away from the design should be curved in such a way that it leads the eye back again.

Linear Pertaining to lines.

Liner A fine pointed brush used for detail work such as lines and branches etc.

Lint *Enemy!* Comes off cloths used to clean, clothing, especially woollens, from hair and rugs or carpets and just in the atmosphere. Look at a shaft of sunlight! Found everywhere (dust and lint that is, not the sunlight)—in the paint, on the painted surface etc. Lint and dust particles landing on a wet area where no further work is to be done before firing usually burn off in the kiln and so are best left alone. While the painting is still being worked these particles gather colour and paint and do cause unsightly marks. Be scrupulously clean with all the tools of trade at all times.

Liquid Bright Gold A liquid gold used to decorate and which is available in varying strengths or percentages from 6% to 24%. However, for painting, a 12% gold content is recommended. Once the jar is opened the contents will thicken with the exposure to air or if it has been stored for some time. This increased viscosity makes the gold more suitable for relief surfaces or rims, as it does not run as easily as the thinner solution. It is possible to thin the liquid gold with gold thinner or lavender oil if it becomes too tacky. Try to pour from the bottle only enough for immediate needs. To be used with care on almost any clean surface. It is a bright high shine metallic colour which may be dulled by applying over previously fired pastel paints or onto a matt surface such as one of the texture pastes, bisque or the body of the porcelain where the glaze has been removed. Apply the gold as evenly as possible as a thicker concentration of gold may be obvious after firing. A lower percentage of gold solution may be applied a little thicker than a higher concentration. It may be painted over fired enamels, texture pastes, structure substances, glass, semi-precious stones. If the surface is not clean the gold will fire black or marked. It may be mixed with some lustres to give different effects and also with some paints. If mixed with the gold rubies or purples it gives a much richer colour. Keep a separate brush for gold at all times and clean it in lavender oil. A jar of lavender oil kept solely to clean your gold brushes and applicators, such as toothpicks, satay sticks etc, will soon contain enough gold to use. If this lavender oil solution is painted onto an unpainted surface, it will fire a delicate mauve, the intensity of which is dependant on the amount of gold in the oil. Firing should be in a well ventilated kiln up to about 300°C. The oils and resins in the liquid gold solution burn off in the form of fumes and these could impair the brilliance if they are not vented from the kiln. Too high a temperature will affect the gold and could cause cracking and dulling. Too low a temperature will allow the gold to be rubbed off. (*See* Degussa section). Lustres over Liquid Bright Gold produce interesting variations of colour.

Liquid Bright Palladium   Similar to Liquid Bright Gold and used in the same way. Silver in colour.

Liquid Bright Platinum   Similar to Liquid Bright Gold. Silver in colour and does not tarnish.

Liquid Burnishing Gold   A liquid gold paint which must be burnished after firing.

Lithographic pencil   Used for drawing on porcelain. These lines will fire off or disappear with the heat of the kiln.

Loading a brush   A brush should be conditioned before use by working oil well into the hairs. Pull the brush along a tile fanning it out a little. If there is not enough oil on the brush it may 'split' or separate. A square shader should be flat when loaded with oil. Load with colour by working into the edge of the pile of mixed paint in a circular or 'C' stroke. This will give you a shaded load with an even distribution of paint across the brush, more intense on the left side if you are a right handed painter, fading to the right.

Local colour   Actual colour of object.

Lost line   The separation or division within a design which is lost because of the common value and tone of two objects, eg a white moth on a cream flower.

Lustre   Solutions of mineral pigments in organic solvents which give an iridescent glaze when applied to porcelain. These liquid metals are not absorbed into the glaze during the firing process and, instead, remain on the surface as does gold. Prior to firing, all the different colours appear brown and are hard to distinguish one from another. Lustres should be stored in a cool dry place in well sealed bottles and cleanliness is essential as dust and moisture will cause marks on the finished surface. Even humid conditions can adversely affect the results. Care must be taken not to contaminate one colour with another or with other products as they lose their colour. The porcelain to be painted should be cleaned with methylated spirits or acetone, not turpentine, and dried with lint free material. For sketching do not use a grease pencil as it will act as a resist and the lustre will not adhere where the pencil has been used. Use a separate brush, cotton tip or sponge for each colour. Pour a little into a small container or dish and do not return to bottle. Take care not to mix or confuse the lids of bottles and to replace the lid on its original bottle as soon as possible as the lustre will collect dust or may tip over. Thickened or jellied lustre may be thinned with lustre thinner or lavender oil preferably in a small dish and not in the bottle, but this is not always successful. A thin coating of the lustre is all that is required for each application and brush strokes should not overlap. Thick applications may well blister and brush off. If penwork is required in the same firing, use an agglutinate mixture of sugar and water as oils will affect the lustre. Enamels and pastes can be applied over unfired lustres but may take on some of the colour. To tint the inside of a cup or box, pour in a few drops and rub with a small pad. When applying lustre with the aid of an air brush, thin a little first. Take care not to touch the unfired lustre as fingerprints can easily be seen and tissues will stick to wet lustre. Moisture from sneezing or coughing can mar the finish.

Bisque painted with lustre has a rich appearance. Fire in an initially ventilated kiln so that the fumes from the oils and resins in the lustre do not mar its brilliance. Colour combinations will give dramatic effects but are subject to many variables such as amount of each lustre used, heaviness of application, firing time, state of lustres etc. Some common combinations:

Copper over pearl = a peacock blue.
Liquid Bright Silver with ruby or purple = maroon.
Yellow pearl over Liquid Bright Silver = bronze.
Blue over fired gold = a gunmetal colour.
Light green over copper bronze = iridescent green.
Yellow over fired orange = auburn.
Pearl over ordinary black paint = satin black.

A marbelising effect can be achieved by applying different lustres to a porcelain surface and dribbling or dabbing with a sponge a little turpentine or lavender oil onto the wet lustre.

Lustres may also be applied to glass in the same manner as to porcelain. Paint with a sheet of white paper behind the glass so that you can see what you are doing.

Lustre resist   Several preparations available from porcelain suppliers. Thick substance resembling poster paint. Water soluble. Apply to white porcelain or over fired lustre. Do not apply over a painted or fluxed surface as it will not come off easily. Sketch design onto surface and paint in areas to be resisted with the lustre resist, eg the petals of flowers, some leaves and stems. Allow to dry. Apply a pale shade of lustre to the entire surface, including the resisted areas. Fire low (700–740°C) as the resist is difficult to remove if fired high. Block in some more flowers with the resist over the pale lustre, allow to dry and apply a further coat of a darker shade of lustre. Fire again. Repeat the process until you have three or four gradually deepening coats of lustre and, after the last fire, wash off the resist with methylated spirits or water. You will have flowers in your design ranging from white through the lustre colours you have used from light to dark.

Majolica   Porous vitreous clay of Hispano-Moresque origin.

Manganese colour   Used in brown and black colours which contain manganese oxide.

Mannerism   A sophisticated and sometimes artificial style of art that evolved from an emotional reaction to the classical rules of the Renaissance.

Marbleising   Application of paint to give the appearance of marble. There are commercial preparations or oils which can be applied to obtain this effect and many other methods which can also be used for the same purpose.
1. Oil is dribbled onto a wet paint surface.
2. Turpentine may be used in the same way.
3. Oil or turpentine may be dribbled onto lustres.
4. Lustres are floated on water and the piece dipped.
5. The wet painted area is dabbed with crushed plastic, foil or other print object.

Masking lacquer   Spirit based resist coating to protect areas of porcelain.

Mass   A coherent body of matter of indefinite shape.

Matt   A dull or satin finish to porcelain.

Matt china   To matt china, use either ivory vellum, matt white or ivory, either mixed with medium and painted on, dusted or lightly grounded.

Matt paints   These paints fire with a satin or matt appearance. Used on bisque porcelain or on surfaces which have been dulled with an application of acid, ivory vellum or have had the glaze removed. Available at porcelain suppliers or it is possible to matt normal powder paints with the addition of zinc oxide. The normal ratio is 4 to 1, however, some powder paints contain a lot of flux and may require more zinc oxide. Liquid detergent used to mix paints will also matt them.

Medium   1. The method in which the artist works: oil, water colour, painting on porcelain.
2. Oil used to apply the paint to the porcelain surface. There are a

Penwork Owl

Gareth
Pen and wash technique

Rose Plate
Soft technique (B. Torkington)

Fruit Bowl
European style (Karen Carter)

Geometric Design
(Barbara Adams)

great number of oils used and even more with which to experiment. The medium should evaporate or volatilise before the glaze melts and the kiln should be well ventilated to prevent the vapour settling on the painted porcelain. The medium should also be able to retain its viscosity during the increasing heat until it evaporates, otherwise it will boil and run before the heat has caused the glaze to melt and absorb the paint, which will flow over the surface with the boiling medium.

Fast drying medium One which dries quickly and is best suited to the rapid painter. *Not* for use in seminars unless a few drops of an open medium are added or the teacher requests it. Main ingredient is usually copaiba.

Slow drying medium For painters who like to take their time and for seminars.

Anise oil Slow drying, light weight oil used for penwork. If too much is used, it may cause the paint to run during the firing process.

Balsam of copaiba Base used for most commercial mediums.

Oil of cloves Slow drying, added to faster drying oils to retard the drying process. If too much is used, it may cause the paint to run in the kiln during the firing process.

Eucalyptus oil Fast drying thin oil, ideal for sgraffito.

Fat oil of turpentine Fast drying oil used in European techniques and in earlier painting methods. Will give body to a medium recipe. *To make*: Place turpentine in a flat dish, cover and leave in a dust free place to evaporate for several weeks.

Kelp oil Slow drying light weight oil used for pen work. If too much is used it may cause the paint to run during the firing process.

Oil of lavender Essential oil used in some mediums as a drying agent. Used in lustre and gold work as well as for painting on bisque.

Spike lavender Less expensive than oil of lavender but has similar properties and is used for the same purposes.

Mineral oil Volatile oil used frequently as a base for open mediums. Could cause loss of colour, chipping and running problems if used too liberally.

Oil of rosemary Used with lustres.

Paraffin oil May be used as a medium as well as to mix paints.

If a medium is too heavy, add drops of either turpentine, lavender, clove or tar oil.

Other oils such as Baby Oil, machine oil, olive oil, motor oil, cooking oil, peanut oil, coconut oil, linseed oil etc can be successful if used with caution. They are mostly volatile oils and boil in the kiln before they evaporate or are burned off, causing the paint to run, lose some colour or chip off. Use very sparingly! See importers and manufacturers sections for brand name mediums.

Glycerine may be used by anyone allergic to various oils or who prefers to paint with a water based medium, to both mix paints and as a painting medium. It is possible to use a water based medium for paints as well as an oil based metallic such as lustre in the same fire if time is short. There are a number of commercial water based mediums available.

Medium recipes   Taken from every source I could find.

Fast drying mediums

1. 2 parts fat oil
   2 parts copaiba
   1 part lavender oil
   1 part clove oil

2. 8 parts copaiba
   1 part clove oil
   1 part lavender oil

3. 8 parts copaiba
   2 parts clove oil
   2 parts lavender oil

Heavy medium
6 parts copaiba
1 part clove oil

Open mediums

4. 1 part lavender
   1 part copaiba
   1 part tar oil
   25 drops of clove oil to each
   ounce

5. 1 part copaiba
   3 parts lavender oil

6. 1 oz mineral oil
   2 ozs clove oil
   ¼ oz lavender oil
   ¼ oz oil of tar

7. 1 pint mineral oil
   1 tablespoon clove oil
   1½ tsp lavender oil

8. Equal parts lavender oil, copaiba and tar oil and add 25 drops of clove oil to every ounce.

Commercial mediums (Courtesy of Russell Cowan.)

Lakides and *June Kay* mediums are copaiba based and are reasonably fast drying, making them very desirable in areas which are inclined to be a little dusty.

Jenny's medium is for the painter who requires a little more time to work on her project.

Dresden Water Based Medium is for one fire painting and for painters with allergy problems.

Grinding Oils M30 and *Dresden Grounding Oil* Dresden Grounding Oil dries quicker than M30 and can be ground immediately. It may be mixed with M30 to obtain an intermediate characteristic. Such an oil is M35.

Russell Cowan Pen Oil and *Barbara Dimitri Pen Oil* are both suitable for very fine pen work. They are fast drying pen oils suitable for pen and wash painting and are also suitable for screenprinting.

Meissenware The first hard paste porcelain made in Europe at Meissen.

Mending cement Clean both edges or surfaces thoroughly. Mix mending cement with water and apply to both surfaces. Place together (in position in the kiln is possibly best as it does not stick until fired) and fire to Cone 017. To hold the pieces in position, use kiln furniture or a cord available at ceramic shops, used for firing beads.

Metallic paints Powder paint with a frosted metallic appearance. Good for grounding and hiding faults. Try grounding over a painted design and detailing the result after firing, or grounding a base and painting a design on the frosted background. Underfired metallic paint will rub off. Fire 750–800°C (1400–1475°F.)

Middleground The area between back and foreground. There is no distinct line drawn between the three areas. Foreground is sharp and clear in detail; background is hazy and indistinct to imply distance; middleground has some broken sharp detail with some indistinct areas and slightly blurred design.

Mildew Dark or black spots which appear in some china. Attributed to bisque being moist when glaze applied. These spots usually fire out when fired very high.

Mille-fiori Italian term for many flowered.

Misting To apply paint with an airbrush or spray can.

Mixed media More than one type of painting material or substance used to create a painting, i.e. paints, glass and texture pastes.

Mixing colours There are so many colours available that it is seldom necessary to mix them dry. However, it is often a good practice to add a little of the main colour featured in your design to some of the background colours, on the brush, to carry the tone through the painting. For instance, if painting in rubies, an addition of ruby colour will 'grey' the darks and give strength to the painting. Try tipping the greys and greens of foliage with a ruby/grey mix. There are many lists of combinations in the various books published.

Mode Form or style.

Modelling Manipulating clay to form a shape or to simulate a form. In our work, one can 'model' the lights and darks to give impressions of concave and convex surfaces (on a petal or part of a body), or the outline of a leaf or flower to change its shape. Porcelain clay can also be formed into an extension of the porcelain blank.

Monochromatic The use of different shades, tones and tints of one colour only. *See* diagram on page 74.

Monochrome To paint the design in a shade of grey or a greyed colour to establish form and values before applying colour. Once the

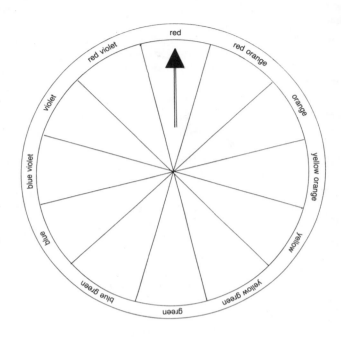

Monochromatic colour scheme

shaded monochrome painting is complete it may be dusted with normal colours before firing or fired as is and painted with washes of colour at a second or third firing stage.

Monogram Two or more intertwined initials.

Mortar Hard vessel in which paints may be ground or pounded with a pestle.

Mosaic A decoration made up of small pieces of various coloured materials positioned to form a pattern. Penwork lines around small painted areas would simulate this effect.

Motif Dominant idea or theme of design or composition. A repeated design.

Motion Or movement . . . a design will be more 'alive' if it appears to have movement within it. For instance, a bird or two in a scene will give life and movement to a painting. Flowers will appear more realistic if they are painted in different positions and facing in different directions. Turning leaves on their side and having suggested forms will help.

Moulding 1. Forming a shape from clay by hand.
2. Pouring slip into a mould to form a shape.

3. Moulding the contour of a petal or leaf with heavy and light applications of paint or with shading.

Movement   An illusion created by the artist to give the effect of a living, vibrant scene, figure or blossom.

Muffle kiln   A low temperature kiln used for firing overglaze colours.

Moll   To pulverise mineral paint with a glass muller and grinding glass.

Muller   Rounded stone or glass grinding tool useful for grinding grainy paints and pigments, preferably on a ground glass tile.

Naturalism   Faithful representation of nature or reality.

Naturalistic   Artist's realistic impression of nature.

Naturalistic design   Nature has provided a wealth of material from which to obtain designs. Vegetables such as capsicum, onion, tomato, enlarged photos of human tissue, land forms and geographical designs and more recently the wonderful photos of the planet from space are wonderful sources of inspiration.

Neoclassic   Return to, revival or adaptation of the classical.

Neo impressionism   Art theory to make impressionism more precise in form. Pointillism painting technique.

Neutral   Not distinctly coloured.

Neutralised colour   Colour which has been greyed.

Nib   Normal ink nibs are used for penwork. A fine mapping pen nib is ideal.

Nonobjectivism   Extreme abstract art which eliminates all recognisable objects.

Notes   What you should keep about every piece you paint. A notebook in your box of tricks is worth its weight in gold if you use it. When you paint anything note the colours used. If you make up a texture paste, note its ingredients, and if you use one colour on top of another in a subsequent fire, note that as well. You may want to know later. If you change the temperature at which you fire, make a note. If something 'strange' comes out of your kiln, note where it was positioned. (You will already have a note as to what it was painted with, won't you?)

Nuggetting   Glass is applied to porcelain with the aid of flux and fired; because the glass contracts at a faster rate than the glaze of the porcelain it will chip off easily during the cooling, taking some of the body of the porcelain with it, leaving a pitted surface. This may then be lustred or coloured.

Sandra Brown hint: Paint nuggeted area with Mother of Pearl lustre before applying Liquid Bright Gold as this will seal the clay body.

Large pieces of glass placed too close together may cause structural fractures during the firing process.

Nyon designs   From Nyon on Lake Geneva. Clear well defined florets in repetitive geometric pattern on white background.

Objective colour   A colour which is called after the object it depicts, eg sky blue, grass green etc.

Objectivism   An art theory stressing objective reality. The exact rendering of detail.

Oil of cloves   Used to prevent colours from drying too rapidly or to 'keep the paint open'.

Oil of lavender   Used to keep colour open, for gold application and to clean brushes used for gold. Used for painting on bisque.

Oil of tar   Mainly used with raised paste for gold to make it more stringy and pliable.

Oil of turpentine   A solvent for cleaning brushes and palette. It may also be used for thinning mixed paints and for applying paint to the surface of the china. However, paint applied this way dries rapidly.

One fire technique   The aim is to obtain the entire design, with full depth of colour with just one application of paint and one firing only. Using a fairly open medium and a comparatively dry brush, paint the design in rich, fully loaded strokes of colour, making each brush stroke count. Either a 'wipe out' or 'paint in' method may be used, with a complete background and sharp accents of depth under the focal areas. Use wet on wet technique to introduce secondary and supporting design. Do not have the medium oil too thick as it will run in the kiln and the thick applications of paint may not be fully absorbed by the glaze and could chip off. A fun exercise to loosen up.

Onglaze   Painting on a glazed surface.

Oozles   The results of turpentine dribbled through paint. (Water colour term.)

Opacifier   Substance which makes a glaze opaque, eg tin, titanium or zirconium.

Opaque porcelain   Hard dense earthenware, similar to ironstone.

Open   A medium is said to be 'open' if it is slow drying. Some never seem to dry.

Outline painting   A simple teaching method. The outline of the flower or design is drawn with a fine liner dipped only in turpentine and mixed paint, the colour usually being of the same tone as the flower, ie ruby for cyclamen, fuchsia or clematis etc, or in the case of white flowers a grey shaded with the tones of the desired background, ie blue, mauve or pink etc. Once the design is drawn, a square shader loaded only with medium is used flat to thin the outline and in doing so bring in enough colour from it to form the shading and moulding of the petals or shapes being painted. Initial lines should not be so heavy that too much paint is carried into the shaded areas but should be thick enough to have sufficient colour to give light shading. The result should be a soft blending of colour giving a delicate moulding and translucent appearance. Ideal for fragile flowers, skin tones, contemporary designs. .

Overglaze Glaze applied over painted design or previously applied glaze.

Overglaze colour Suitable colour for painting on a glazed surface.

Oversights The 'nasties' you fired onto your porcelain because you did not check it properly.

Over-tint Application of colour over an already fired painted area.

Overwork Paint which has been pushed and pulled around the plate will fire dull and grainy.

Oxide Compound of oxygen with another element or with a radical (an element or atom or group of these, which forms the base of a compound and remains unchanged during ordinary chemical reactions).

Padding Blending and softening a design or smoothing an application of oil for grounding by padding or pouncing with a pad made from cotton wool covered with fine silk.

Painting Applying paint consisting of pigments or colours, mixed with a liquid medium such as oil, varnish, milk, glue or water to a surface by brushing, spraying, a variety of tools, a roller or other padded device. The surface to be painted may be paper, canvas, wood, stone, plaster or porcelain.

Palette A covered flat box or tray in or on which to keep your paints. Should be kept clean to prevent the dust particles it attracts from marring your painting.

Palette knife A flat stainless steel blade with a wooden handle which is used for grinding paints and occasionally with care for painting.

Pantograph Drawing device used to enlarge or reduce a design.

Paper doily To reproduce a paper doily pattern, thoroughly paint and pad a plate with grounding oil. Carefully position a paper doily on the surface and dust with dry powder paints. Remove excess and gently lift doily. Ideas may also be obtained for raised paste, enamel and relief pastes.

Paper, painting on It is possible to paint on various types of paper using your porcelain paints and mediums. Plasticised paper, oil painting paper and other oil painting surfaces may be used. A fast drying or

Copaiba based medium is best. Good brush stroke techniques are an advantage as although it is possible to clean the paper with turpentine or lavender oil it is not as easy as porcelain. Once the painting is dry, additional depth and detail may be added, as well as shadow areas over previously painted surfaces with care. Once the painting is finished, it should dry thoroughly, then be sprayed with one of the oil painting lacquers. Waterbased mediums and paint mixed with glycerine may also be used on various types of paper in the same manner.

Paraffin oil Mixture of hydrocarbons obtained by distillation of petroleum. May be used as medium or to mix powder paint. Use with care as too much oil will cause running in the firing process.

Parchment Treated animal skin used for painting and writing.

Paste gold Gold in paste form. Mix to painting consistency with lavender oil, essence or facilitator.

Pat gold A flat smear of gold which is softened with lavender oil, essence or facilitator.

Peduncle Stalk of flower or fruit.

Pen and wash A method of sketching in grey, brown or dark green then washing colour over the design. If the sketch is executed in a simple syrup, the wash may be applied with a normal medium in the same firing stage, as the oil based medium will not move the simple syrup or water based design.

Pen oil A fine thin open medium for use with pen nibs. Various brands available. Or: Thin mixed paint with turpentine to ink consistency. Mix powder paints with simple syrup, sugar based soft drink such as lemonade, Coca-Cola, Seven Up etc. The diet soft drinks are not based on sugar and therefore do not work.

Penwork Penning a design with a nib. A mapping pen, an ink composed of paint pigments and a prepared surface are the requirements.

Perspective The impression of distance and depth.

Step 1
Draw a horizontal line in pencil.

Vanishing
Point

Vanishing
Point

Step 2
Cross it with a vertical line in ink.

Step 3
Draw line from V.P. to both ends of vertical line in pencil.

Step 4
Add vertical lines for breadth and depth of building (pencil).
Connect vertical lines.

Step 5
Find ceiling height.

Step 6
Add a verandah. Ink in outline.

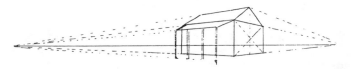

Step 7
Erase pencil marks.

Step 8
Embellish.
Think of source of light.
Shadow accordingly.

Simple perspective drawing.

Petal   Each of the divisions of the corolla of a flower.

Petit point   Painting with texture to resemble tapestry. Choose a piece of porcelain with a convex surface and tautly cover with a piece of fine nylon net, securing with an elastic band or clothes peg. Make sure all the net lines are straight. Apply petit point paste evenly (thinned with turpentine if necessary) with a brush leaving the net visible. Allow to dry naturally and remove net. Fire to manufacturer's instructions or around 780–800°C. Sand gently and paint with matt paints as for bisque. The net may be re-used!

Petit point paste   Substance with dull matt finish which gives the petit point texture. Usually pre-mixed. Powdered colour may be added in small proportions. Fired at 780–800°C. Porous after firing and colours and metallics will fire dull when applied over the paste.

Photography   Photographing porcelain can be difficult and disappointing. There is a wide range of cameras and equipment available and you should familiarise yourself with your own. A good lens will let you get close enough to 'fill the frame' with the object you want to photograph. The background for your porcelain should be uncluttered and not divided by the edge of a table or shelf. I like a black drape for most porcelain with most of the drape area excluded, otherwise it will wash out the colour on the porcelain piece. I have found blue intrusive and neutral colours seem to blend too well without giving contrast. If you want to have your work reproduced, transparencies are better than negatives. However, it is a good idea to send a print as well (if only to stop them printing your work upside down). Try not to use a flash so as to avoid the reflection and also be wary of reflections from windows, trees, people and of course, the photographer. Photographs taken outside in early morning or evening daylight before the sun washes out some of the colour seem to be successful. Take at least two or three photographs of each object. It is not really advisable to spray your porcelain with hairspray or commercial varieties of spray. If there is a gold trim it could be marred, or enamel could be chipped off. It is possible to take good photographs without that precaution.

Piece   Object to be painted. China blank.

Pigment   Colouring in paints or dyes.

Pistil   Ovulating organ of a flower.

Plate divider   A pattern or template to divide a plate into sections for a repetitive design. *See* diagram on next page.

Plate rack   Kiln furniture designed to hold plates in a vertical position during firing.

Plate stand   Different types of plate stand are illustrated on the next page.

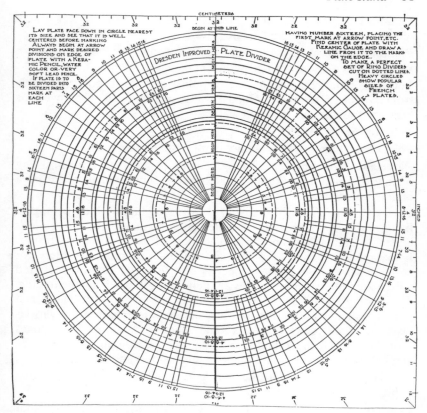

Plate divider, about one-quarter actual size

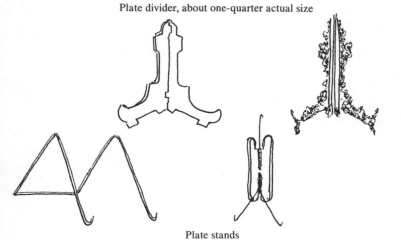

Plate stands

Platinum   A rare metallic element, fusable only at very high temperatures. Treat as you would gold.

Pointillism   Painting with small coloured dots which blend when viewed from a distance to give tonal and colour values.

Polishing sand   Fine sand used to polish or burnish gold. Available from porcelain suppliers. Good results are obtained when work is burnished submerged in warm water.

Polychrome   Multi-coloured.

Polyptych   Painting or sculpture in more than three panels.

Porcelain   The finest and hardest kind of earthenware consisting mainly of china clay (kaolin) or felspathic clay, fired or baked at a high temperature.

Portraits   The (usually realistic) painting of faces which belong to living subjects. There are commercially prepared portrait colours available, although it is possible to use normal paints with good results. It is probably better to paint with an open medium to allow for corrections. Acetate tracing paper is best for clear transparency and a light graphite paper and stylus are helpful for transferring the tracing. The tracing should show all the main detail lines of eyes, nose and mouth. Another invaluable tool is a compass to measure the various distances, such as width of eyes and space between, etc. Skin tones should be smooth and rounded. To obtain a good resemblance, carefully and faithfully reproduce the shape of all shadows and highlights.

Pouncing   A cottonwool-filled silk pad is bounced on a painted area to blend and soften the colours.

Powdered glaze   Heavily fluxed powder. Mix with soft pastel colour using any medium and apply to porcelain surface. Pad with silk pad. The more glaze powder mix left on the surface the higher the glaze, however too much will 'eat' the colours applied both before and after. Fire at a lower temperature if you have this problem.

Practise   To work at perfecting an ability, like piano playing. If you do not practise, you will not be able to paint well.

Pre-tint   Wash of colour applied to the painting surface and fired prior to the design being painted.

Preserving varnish   Varnish applied as a liquid which sets to area which is to be kept white or previously painted colour while surrounding area is painted, dusted or grounded and which is then removed before firing. If fired it will adhere to the surface as a raised roughened texture (suitable for tree trunks and other roughened effects).

Pricking   Method of transferring a design by means of a series of dots which are then joined up.

Primary colours The primary colours of pigmented paints are *red,* *yellow* and *blue.*

Printing Painting a shape or object such as a leaf with paint, lustre (work quickly with lustre), gold or texture paste and 'stamping' the porcelain surface with it. If you use a texture paste, it may then be painted with paint, lustre or gold etc.

Proportion Comparative relationship. Objects within your design should relate in size both to each other and to the porcelain blank. All parts of a floral design should match in size. If you are painting roses three inches in diameter, all the blooms should be approximately that size, not the main one three inches and the subordinate ones one and a half inches, only because they are less important. In landscapes trees retreating into the distance are smaller in stature, not the same size as the ones in the foreground. Pears, apples, oranges should be relative in size to grapes, cherries, etc.

Publish To submit work to a magazine for publication. If you would like to have your work published there are a number of magazines which will accept articles especially if you are a subscriber. I know of no porcelain art magazine that will pay you for your article, however there are some art and craft magazines which do. Your work must be original or you must have the authority of the author or artist and the credit is given to that person. If you submit something done in a seminar situation, this also should be stated. Do not send the original work and do not discredit your efforts with inferior photography. Professional photography is expensive and sometimes an amateur produces better results with a little effort. Send transparencies as opposed to negatives unless otherwise requested and enclose colour prints as well to help the editor select size and placement etc. It is always advisable to send a stamped addressed envelope to ensure their return. Use black and white photography only if there is good contrast and clear precise linear work. The photographs should be clearly labelled showing which way is up, the title and your name. They should be accompanied by an explanatory text which should be concise and yet contain all relevant information: your reasons for painting that particular subject on that particular blank, how you went about it, the materials used and the temperature at which it was fired. An article which rambles on will be cut or if too terse may be overlooked.

Pure colour The colour without additives.

Pyrometer An instrument to measure the temperature inside the kiln during firing.

Pyrometric cones Clay pyramids used to show the temperature in a kiln. *See* illustration on page 61.

Quadrant system   Dividing the china into four sections to plan design.

Quartz   A mineral consisting of silicon dioxide.

Queen's ware   Cream earthenware made by Wedgwood for Queen Charlotte.

Quill   A pen or brush resembling the quill of a feather.

Raised enamels   Enamel applied to form a relief design. *See* enamel.

Raised paste   A paste applied to china in relief as a base for Roman Gold. May be purchased in a pre-mixed state, either white which fires with a satin finish or yellow which fires semi matt. Colour may be added to the white paste, but not to the yellow, and it may be painted after firing. White raised paste is suitable for Liquid Bright Gold, Platinum or Bronze. Yellow raised paste will take these metallics plus Burnishing, Matt and Roman Gold. The powdered paste may be mixed with medium for raised paste and turpentine, painting medium, water-based mediums, fat oil and turpentine, and copaiba. Experiment with other liquids for different effects. Do not use grounding oils, glycerine or mineral based open mediums as these may cause the paste to flatten and crack. Oil of tar may be added to give body to the paste and help it to 'string'. Pastes are porous after firing and care should be taken to keep them clean so as not to contaminate the gold when it is applied.

To mix: Place a quantity of powder on a ground glass slab and, using a glass muller or bone knife, mix with alcohol and grind the powder until quite dry. Use enough oil or raised paste medium to bind it and add a little oil or tar. It should be crumbly not thin. Moisten with turpentine, heating gently if possible and continue to stir, testing the stringing ability after five or ten minutes. If it does not string add a little more oil of tar until it does. Paste for dots should not have too much oil of tar added. Fire at 780–820°C normally; however fire only as high as necessary to mature gold or colour if successive firings are required. Damp or rainy weather is not conducive to good raised paste, as the moisture in the air affects the properties of the paste.

Method: Place an amount of Hancock's paste onto a tile and divide into 8 even sections. Add ⅛ (the same amount as one of the portions of paste) tin oxide and add just enough copaiba medium to hold the mixture together, plus a drop of fat oil. Mix until crumbly. Add a few drops of turpentine and continue to mix, breathing warm air on it, until it 'strings', usually ten or so minutes.

Raw glaze   Unfritted glaze.

Realism   Accurate representation of nature or real life subjects.

Realistic   Painting which is a true representation of the study or model.

Reducing glass   The opposite of a magnifying glass which will often help identify obvious faults in design.

Reduction glaze A glaze which will develop and mature its colour in a reducing atmosphere.

Reflected light The light bounced back onto one object from another.

Refractory Able to resist high temperature. A heat resistant substance that raises the melting temperature of a glaze, eg flint, quartz, tin oxide, titania, chrome, zirconia and antimony.

Relief Method of moulding, carving or stamping in which design stands out from plane or curved surface. Low or high relief.

Relief white Powder which is mixed with medium and fires in opaque relief. Some are porous, others not as porous, depending on the brand. The higher the fire, the more glossy the result. Like most relief pastes it does not like repeated firings.

Repetition A design which is repeated more than once.

Resist Used to cover a portion of the porcelain surface to protect it from the other techniques used to decorate the piece, eg grounding, lustre etc. There are several substances with different properties available. See manufacturers' lists to find one to suit your needs.

Rhythm Pleasing design with sense of balance and movement.

Roman Gold A burnishing gold paste with a higher concentration of gold than the liquid golds. May be fluxed for use on an unpainted porcelain surface or unfluxed for use on a painted surface.

Romanesque Italian style characterised by sweeping arches and heavy ornamentation.

Rookwood The original Rookwood technique was an underglaze design; however, today it refers to a highly glazed surface with the design deeply embedded and coloured with overtones of one colour. Briefly, the design is sketched on and painted in a monochrome with stronger contrasts and heavier accents than normal, but with care taken to see that there are no build ups of paint. This is fired and future firings consist of various methods of applying layers of one or two colours over the monochrome painting. Washes of colour and dusting are the most common with yellow and red being the most popular combination.

Rouging As blushing. A small amount of colour is picked up on the finger tip and rubbed into the design to tint it or give it colour. Dampen the finger tip first with medium.

Ruby colours Very high in gold content and therefore very expensive. Fire over 800°C to mature.

Rustiban *Caution.* Weak solution of hydrofluoric acid which must be used with great caution to remove fired paint from porcelain. It is a commercial preparation normally used to remove rust stains from clothing. If only a small area of the design is to be removed, resist the surrounding area with masking lacquer, lustre resist, or even nail polish and, using rubber gloves, paint the area with the solution on a cotton bud. Allow it to penetrate the glaze and the colour will gradually be removed. Wash off thoroughly when colour is completely stripped. The area will be etched because the glaze has been removed. A wash of clear or white paint or a coat of Crystal Glaze will help to bring back some of the gloss. If the whole object is to be treated, place in a plastic container of water, add Rustiban (the amount will depend on the size of container and how rapidly the colour is to be removed—½ the Rustiban container to a four gallon bucket would be a rough measure) and leave immersed in the solution for a week or so. Several pieces may be immersed at once or, if a tall narrow object, space may be taken up with a lidded plastic container full of water or a brick in order to have a more concentrated solution. *Caution: Wear protective clothing and gloves* whenever using acid. If acid splashes onto skin wash immediately with soap and a soda solution as the resultant burn could be very severe. Seek medical attention if this is the case.

S curve   Pleasing line of design in the shape of an S.

Sabatella   Commercially prepared medium used for grinding and painting. Very open and has to be used very sparingly otherwise colours will run and separate.

Sagger   Fire clay case used to protect porcelain objects in the kiln from flames and fumes.

Salt glaze   A glaze formed by the introduction of raw salt to the kiln at 2300°F. The vapour combines with the clay's silica to form the glaze.

Sand   May be used in a number of ways. Naturally coloured sands will adhere to the porcelain when applied with a mix of flux and medium. Fired quite high, this mix may be used to create scenes, designs etc. Neutral sand may be painted once it is fired onto the porcelain, or powdered paint may be mixed with the flux and sand and applied as a coloured texture. If the sand is not in direct contact with the glaze it will brush off after firing, as will any surplus sand.

Sand blasting   The removal of the surface of porcelain with sand or grit forced from an air blaster. There are various grades of grit used and the pressure is approximately 40 lbs of dry air. It should be used in a well ventilated area and a mask should be worn to prevent inhalation of the dust particles. Draw the design onto the porcelain blank and colour in the part to be etched with a spirit based felt pen. The sand blaster is held about an inch away from the china and moved across the coloured in surface. Once all the colour is removed the

Modern Techniques
Use of stones, glass and texture
pastes

Wildflowers of Kakadu
Texture pastes, enamels, glass
and lustres

The Voyeur
Modern techniques using texture
pastes, enamels, glass and lustres
(Photography A. Patten)

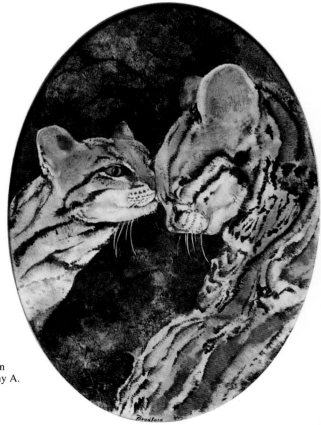

Mother Love
Painted on porcelain
canvas (Photography A.
Patten)

etching should be complete and the piece may be thoroughly cleaned, dried and painted with lustres or gold etc. The airbrush may also be used to apply the solutions.

Sang-de-boeuf This term of French origin describes a vivid red Chinese glaze derived from copper oxides.

Satsuma A soft crackled Japanese ware.

Scale Drawing or painting to scale is important. The relative size of objects such as fruit, e.g. pears and strawberries, violets and daisies, eyes in a face, all indicate correct proportions.

Schira diluent Thinners used by Georges Miserez Schira.

Schira medium Medium used for one fire European style painting.

Scroller A fine long haired brush which comes to a point.

Scrolling May also be penned in gold, silver, lustres or paint.

Scrolls Decoration consisting of comma shapes in either pen work or relief paste. Push a pen nib stylus or brush tip into a mound of mixed paste and lift in an upward motion. Poise the nib or brush above the surface so that the paste barely comes in contact with the porcelain. Draw the shape towards you and the paste will pull out in a tapering comma shape in the direction of the follow through. Lift the brush or nib away from the surface to end the movement.

Secondary colours Made from equal amounts of primary colours, ie equal parts of red and yellow will produce orange; equal parts of yellow and blue will produce green and equal parts of red and blue will produce violet.

Selenium Used in low fire red colours.

Seminar A short one, two or three day course in a certain subject. Attend as many as you are able. You will always learn something, even if only what not to do. Seminars are not always easy to arrange and much time is spent in preparation by the instructors, who disrupt their own schedule to give the seminar. Some thought should be given to this by people who thoughtlessly cancel late or who do not turn up.

Semi porcelain Ironstone like earthenware.

Sepal Leaflike division of calyx of flower. *See* diagram on page 23.

Sevres Originally soft then hard paste porcelain from the town of Sevres in France.

Sfumato The blending of outlines and forms to give a soft atmospheric or smoky effect.

Sgraffito A design which has been scratched out of paint, slip or glaze.

Shade Colour to which black or some other colour has been added. Absence of bright light.

Shaded load Load the brush across its entire width, then partially side load it with a darker shade or value of the same colour.

Shadow Area furthermost from light source.

Shadow area Area not in path of light source.

Shadow leaves The cast shadow of leaves or flowers not necessarily in the design.

Shaping up technique Outlining a form with brushstrokes to give it shape and body.

Shrinkage A piece of fired ware is smaller in size than the raw clay because the moisture content is evaporated and the clay particles move closer together.

Side load Load the brush with a circular motion into the paint, until the paint is spread two thirds across the width of the brush.

Simili incrustation The decoration of edges with matt firing colours or gold base coats.

Simple syrup For penwork. Mix 1 part icing sugar, 1 part water and 2 parts powder paint. Use with mapping pen. An even simpler syrup is made by mixing your powder paints with a sugar based soft drink such as Coca-Cola, Seven Up etc. Do not use artificially sweetened liquids.

Slip Clay with a high water content and creamy consistency used for making, cementing, colouring and decorating clay bodied wares.

Slip casting Slip or liquid clay is poured into a plaster mould, which leaches moisture from it so that clay is then deposited onto the walls of the mould. Excess slip is poured off.

Soaking Maintaining the temperature of a kiln for a length of time to allow the heat to fully penetrate the pieces being fired.

Soft paste porcelain Simulated porcelain fired at a low temperature. Usually glazed with tin.

Soft ware Porcelain clay to which flux has been added.

Solvent Material used to dissolve a substance.

Split-complementary Colour combination made up of a key colour and two colours adjacent to its complementary colour. *See* diagram on next page.

Sponge work Application of colour with the aid of a sponge. The mixed paint is thinned slightly with turpentine and applied by padding

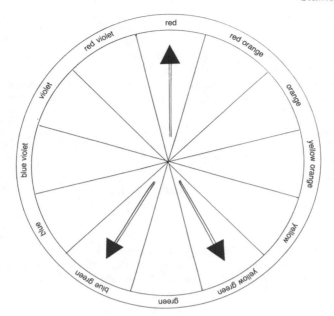

Colour wheel showing split-complementary colours

the colour onto the object to be painted with plastic sponge. The application should not be too heavy or it will chip off. It is better to apply several coats, firing between each for a rich, even colour. Suitable for borders, areas of solid colour, stencil motifs, or a design may be 'wiped' from the applied colour.

Spun glass burnisher Burnishing brush consisting of fibres of spun glass. It is used for burnishing gold.

Square shader Brush which varies in width from 1 millimetre to five or so centimetres. The bristles also vary in length and are long and straight.

Stain A prepared and fritted colouring agent for slips, glazes, overglazes etc.

Stamen Male fertilising organ of flowering plants, with anther containing pollen supported on slender footstalk. *See* diagram on page 13.

Stamp   A shape may be used as a stamp to print colour onto the painting surface by sponging a coat of colour onto a small area on your tile and using it as a stamp pad. Another method is to use a grounding oil or thick quick drying medium as a stamp pad and press the stamp into it and then onto the china; wait for several minutes until touch dry but still a little tacky and dust with the desired colour. Brush off excess dust and fire.

Stamping gold   A bright gold used for stamping a design on china. Available as a paste or in liquid form which must evaporate a little prior to use. Liquid Bright Gold may be used if allowed to thicken for a few minutes by exposing to air. The paste is thinly spread on a glass slab, stamped with a rubber stamp and transferred to the porcelain. The liquid is used in the same manner. The stamp is usually of embossed rubber.

Stencil motifs   A simple shape is sketched onto card or thick paper and cut out. You will now have a 'shape' and a 'negative shape' or card which has a hole in it the shape of the object you have drawn. Place the card with the cut out hole onto the porcelain and colour the exposed surface by painting, pouncing with a sponge dipped in mixed paint or air brushing. Alternatively, place the cut out shape on the porcelain and paint, sponge or air brush colour around it. The motif may be repeated as often as desired to form the design. Combine the two for interesting effects.

Still life   Painting of a subject that once had life.

Stilts   Supports for glazed objects during firing.

Stippling   A 'broken' look achieved by tapping wet painting with a flat deersfoot or similar brush.

Stoneware   Hard dense pottery made from siliceous clay or a mixture of clay, flint and sand.

Strasbourg   European design in the style created in the factories of the city of Strasbourg.

String Not, in this case, a piece of twine. It is a verb meaning to cause the enamel or paste to elongate or 'draw out'. The enamel or paste which is being carried on the stylus is touched to the porcelain surface and as the stylus is lifted the paste will stay in contact with the porcelain and be pulled along by the stylus in the desired direction. If it 'strings' well, the shapes will be long and well formed without lumps and air bubbles and without breaking.

Study A design used as a guide or pattern.

Style The techniques used in a particular method of painting or the characteristic painting traits of an individual.

Stylised flowers As in European style painting. Not photo realistic.

Stylus In our case, a pointed tool used for tracing, paste work, drawing in unfired paint and placing pieces of glass or decoration in position.

Subject The feature of your painting. Study and know it well. Look at as many photographs, drawings and interpretations of the real thing as possible. And the object itself if convenient. Know its anatomy, habits, colours, varieties, anything at all of interest to give your own rendering realism and life. Even an abstract painting caricatures realism.

Sugar painting Mix four parts powder paint to one part icing sugar with a little water to ink consistency. It dries quickly so you will have to keep adding water. Work rapidly and apply your design either in a paint in method or apply paint for a wipe out design. With the paint in method make every brush stroke exactly where you want it as it is not possible to blend as easily as when painting with oil. With the wipe out method, remove the colour from your brush with water and lift the paint from the areas of the design with the water moistened brush. The piece may be fired or with care a second layer of paint may be applied for depth and detail, such as stamens on flowers, veins on leaves etc. Take care not to apply the paint too thickly otherwise it will chip off. It is difficult to eliminate brush strokes and blending is not always possible. Wash brushes well; however, they may retain grains of paint and sugar and should not be used for normal painting techniques as they may leave deposits.

Surrealism Movement in art purporting to express the subconscious activities of the mind and usually resulting in grotesque and imaginative symbolism.

Talent The ability or aptitude to execute (in our case) an art form easily. Very few people are natural artists and those who are credited with having talent usually work hard to develop it. We mere mortals need a great deal of assistance, practice and patience.

Tar, oil of An oil used as a medium. It can also be added to raised paste to assist in its application.

Teacher   A teacher has to know more than the student and to be able to execute it better. A *good* teacher is something else again. Teachers should have a knowledge of art, colour, materials used and be versatile in their abilities, not only as painters but also in being able to impart and share the skills and knowledge they have acquired. They have also to be amateur psychologists. Most States in Australia have an association which is a stepping stone towards teaching and aspiring artists are advised to join one of these groups to increase their own ability and to learn of some of the problems that go with teaching and how others have handled them. NSW has T.I.P.A.; in Victoria, aspiring teachers join A.P.A.T. as Associate Teachers for one year and must then submit work for assessment. South Australia has a Teachers' Association to which artists apply and Western Australian TAFE Colleges include onglaze painting in their Diploma of Art and Design courses. There are prerequisites for joining all these associations or courses. There is also an organisation known as A.P.A.T., Australasian Porcelain Art Teachers Association for teachers to meet and discuss methods, different techniques, hold workshops and once every two years organise a major exhibition to which many international artists come to share their knowledge, demonstrate and give seminars. In the alternate year each State has its own prestigious exhibition. This Association is recognised internationally and to become a member, a porcelain artist must have taught continuously, with at least five pupils, for two years, be proposed by two existing members and, depending on the various State rules, pass an assessment. Other international organisations such as International Porcelain Art Teachers and World Porcelain Artists are available for teachers and each has its own merits. It is advisable for students to look for an accredited teacher if they have the opportunity.

Tempera   Painting with pigments or colours which have been mixed with a natural emulsion such as egg yolk or artificial emulsion such as oil and gum.

Tertiary colours   Equal parts of secondary colours and one primary colour.

Test tile   It is always a good idea to know the materials you use and test tiles are designed to show you the colour of the paint pigments, how they blend with each other, how they fire at various temperatures, how and if they mix with other products. *See* pages 33 and 34.
To make a sample test tile:
1. Paint a shaded stroke of all your blue paints right across a tile leaving the top half inch. Write in their brand names to identify them and fire. Then paint another stroke of all your pinks, roses and rubies down the tile, starting in the unpainted area at the top and leaving

an area of the original blue showing down the left side of the tile. Identify these colours as well and fire. You will now have a record of all your blues, pinks and a range of mauves and purples you did not know you owned. Make tiles of other useful colour combinations such as autumn tones, blues and greens etc.

2. Prepare a test tile of all your enamels and pastes, without the addition of colour pigments and foreign substances such as sand and glass. Label well, allow to dry and fire. Note results in pen ink on the tile and fire again, this time to test the tolerance of the enamels to further firings. On a separate tile, fired concurrently, try the various additives such as sand, glass and colour and note these reactions as well. Experiment with size and height.

3. Prepare a test tile of your texture pastes as for enamels.

4. Lustres provide another opportunity to make a test tile and diagonal bands may also be added to the lattice pattern previously described. Also prepare a sample of the same lustre applied upon itself several times, firing between each layer. Experiment and save the results for future reference.

Texture   Texture is both visual and tactile. It may be obtained by a variety of methods. To obtain a visual effect try brushstrokes, stippling, mottled colours etc, and for a tactile effect use one of the many commercial preparations available, such as Texture Coat, Ruff-It, Petit Point Paste, Base for Raised Gold, enamel etc and of course the addition of sand, glass, stones and other solid matter which tolerates heat.

Texture coat   White powder which may be mixed with most liquids, ie medium, milk, sugar solutions, glycerine etc. It will react differently with each one and according to the various firing temperatures and the stiffness or liquidity of the mixture. It may be applied by brush, sponge, pen, print etc and may be coloured with the addition of about $1/6$ or $1/8$ of dry powder paint. It may also be painted after firing. It fires a glossy, semi transparent white without additives and may be fired between 700 and 820°C. The higher the temperature, the flatter the result.

Texture pastes   *Texture Coat, Ruff-It, enamel, Base for Raised Gold, Hancock's Raised Paste, Petit Point Mixture, Dresden Raised Paste* and *Gold Underlay*, etc. There are many textured pastes on the market and each of them is different. Always follow the manufacturers' instructions (where I have been given them, they are listed under the name of the manufacturer) for tried and proven results, however each paste will react according to many variables including the human element. Application, the porcelain, the heat of and the position in the kiln, the amount and type of solution with which it is mixed, the amount of time it has been allowed to dry and numerous other factors must be taken into account.

Some methods of application:
1. Padding with assorted textured sponges and shapes.
2. Thinned textured paste flowed onto an area.
3. Thickened paste padded with wrinkled foil, plastic wrap, paper or cloth.
4. 'Printing' with shaped objects, such as leaves, stamps etc.
5. Pressing with woven fabrics.
6. Drawing through a comb, fork or satay stick at varying times of drying.
7. Flicking off a tooth brush or dropping from a pointer.
8. Pressing with a palette knife.
You are limited only by your own imagination.

Thinking   What you should be doing all the time! However, take a moment to think laterally. Is the way you are going about whatever it is that you are doing the only way? the best way? What are the alternatives?

Tiles   Most tiles have a softer glaze than porcelain and will absorb paint and pastes more readily. They come in various sizes and it is possible to obtain both ceramic and porcelain tiles. Care should be taken when firing tiles to protect them from uneven heat; do not place them against the wall of the kiln close to the exposed elements.

Time/temperature curve   The time take to attain a desired temperature during the firing process. The longer it takes to bring the kiln to the desired temperature, the lower that temperature has to be to mature the products being fired. The more rapidly a kiln is fired, the higher the temperature should be to mature the contents. The length of time that the clay body is subjected to heat determines the maturity of the paints used, not the actual temperature. For instance, if you load your kiln with only two or three pieces and switch it to 800°C and it takes 3 hours to attain that temperature, the paints will react in a certain manner. Then, if you fully load your kiln and switch it to 800°C and it takes 3½ hours, the paints will have been subjected to heat for a longer period and the reaction will differ from the previous example.

Tin colours   Yellows.

Tin glaze   Lead glaze to which tin oxide has been added.

Tin oxide   Used with raised paste to facilitate its application. Use $1/8$ ratio of tin oxide to paste.

Tint   Addition of white to lighten a colour or to darken slightly with a pastel colour the pure white porcelain on which we paint, to give it 'tooth'.

Tondo   Circular painting.

Top loading   Loading two or more colours on top of each other on the brush to create different colour combinations.

Touch dry Unfired paint is touch dry when it no longer feels tacky but there is a slight 'pull' when contact is made.

Trace To make a copy of a subject by placing a sheet of transparent paper over the painting or sketch and drawing the outline and detail which shows through. Tracing should only be used to give beginners confidence and to attain accuracy from your own sketches. You can learn a lot from copying and developing your own techniques and style but very little from continuing to trace. An effective tracing procedure is to place graphite paper the correct side down (test it first) onto the porcelain and place your drawing over the top. Fix in position with adhesive tape. Using a stylus, carefully go over the drawing, making sure all the lines are repeated. When you have finished, remove both the papers and you will have your tracing. (At this stage you may like to lightly dust the transferred design with a pale colour powder paint and fire it. The design will be permanently in situ and ready for further treatment.)

Transparent effect The effect a porcelain painter obtains when applying colours over previously fired colours. For instance a wash of blue over a fired pale green leaf; some of the blue is removed, allowing the original green to show through.

Triadic colour scheme Made up of three colours equidistant on the colour wheel.

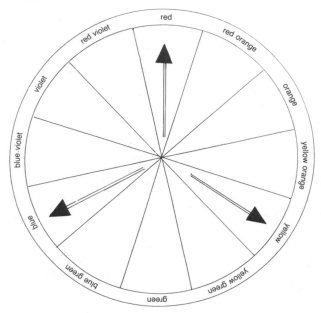

Primary colour triadic colour scheme

Triptych   Painting in three panels.

Trivet   Stand for tiles.

Trompe l'oeil   Painting in which objects appear to be real.

Trunks of trees   Will be easier to sketch or paint if the plate or tile is turned upside down and the trees drawn from the base to the top and 'pulled' towards you. The broader base of the trunk will taper to the division of the branches which can be pulled towards the tips in the same manner. Roughened bark can be applied with textures or marks can be drawn into the wet paint with a stylus or some other tool such as a sponge or twisted hairy ball of twine. Look for all the unusual colours in bark, the reds, blues and greens, and apply them lightly.

Turnback   That part of the petal or leaf which folds over. As a rule it should be lighter in colour than the main part which is darker immediately under the fold because it is in shadow. Most importantly, it should be in proportion to the rest of the leaf or petal and have a straight or slightly concave edge.

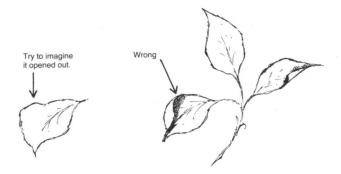

Try to imagine it opened out.

Wrong

Turpentine   Colourless or yellow volatile inflammable oil used to remove unfired paint from painted surface, to clean brushes, to 'repel' paint, as a very fast drying medium to apply paint and as a thinner for mixed paints to be used as a wash; also for signature ink or outline painting. Art turpentine is more expensive but is more pure and has a more agreeable odour than household turpentine.

Alternatives: Waterbased mediums, lavender oil.

Turps repel   Selected paints mixed with medium are applied to the porcelain surface and dabbed with a turpentine soaked brush. The paint will run and dribble over the area as the object is tilted and turned. When dried and fired the shapes and patterns frequently lend themselves to an active imagination. Faces, animals, landscapes can be seen and enhanced with some extra lines and colour in a subsequent firing. Other methods include (a) wetting the surface with turpentine and adding paint, either dry powder or mixed, and letting the colours run or turn; (b) loading a turpentine filled brush with mixed paint and allowing it to flow over the area with movement of the plate or tile; (c) using lustres rather than paints with any of the previously mentioned methods. Paints mixed with different mediums give different results, as do different brands of paint. There are several types of turpentine available and each of these will react differently. The result is entirely unpredictable but a lot of fun.

Underglaze Design applied at the bisque stage prior to application of the glaze.

Unfluxed gold A paste gold which is purchased in the form of a circular pat of paste. For use over a painted surface where there is already flux in the previous coat of paint.

Value Confusing term given many different meanings. Dimension of colour denoting the relative darkness or lightness of a colour. Imagine the colours of a painting as if they were shades of grey in a black and white painting. Could you differentiate between two adjacent colours if they were grey and had no border or outline?

Value glass Used in the manner of a magnifying glass. The colours are reduced to shades of grey and the values can be determined.

Vanadium colours Greens and blues.

Vehicle The liquid which is used for 'grinding' the powdered paint and holding it in suspension.

Viscosity The internal property of a liquid which influences its rate of flow.

Warm colours Yellows, reds and oranges which seem to give the appearance of being closer. To help subdue a dominant portion of the background painted in these colours, give it a wash of a cool colour, such as blue. It will then recede.

Wash of colour The application of colour in broad, flat areas to gently colour a black and white sketch, to push an intruding or displeasing flower or areas of design into the background or highlight part of a design.

Wet on wet Application of paint on freshly applied, unfired paint. To be done with great care as your first stroke will apply paint and this dries rapidly. Your second application will move your first coat of colour unless you exercise caution.

Whink   *Caution*: Product equivalent to Rustiban available in the USA. Diluted hydrofluoric acid used to remove fired painted designs.

Whiskers   Long fine hairs on the cheeks of animals. Very difficult to render realistically as they are so light and fine. Best done with a very fine scroller, mapping pen or rubber tip and thinned even further with the rubber tip. Light or white whiskers are wiped out in the first fire or painted in with fine enamel lines on the last fire after all painting in that area is finished. Dark brown or black whiskers are painted in the last fire either with paint or coloured enamel. Understated whiskers are better than an over-abundance.

White granite   Hard dense porcelain similar to ironstone.

White relief   Thicker than normal white paint which is applied for relief decoration.

Windows of light   Areas of light in the design. Very important. Without these light patches the design would be dull and colourless and the painting would have no contrast.

Wipe out   To remove freshly applied wet paint and produce a design.

Worcester   Porcelain made in the factories in the town of Worcester, England.

Wrico pen   A pen which could be filled with gold or platinum and used for penwork and decoration.

Tools of trade (L to R): 1. Mapping pen. 2. Cerama-Pen (gold or silver). 3. Tool to apply borders to plates. 4, 5. Two types of stylus. 6, 7, 8. Erasers or wipeout tools. 9. Gold applicator with various felt tips. 10. Gold eraser. 11. Fibreglass burnishing brush. 12. Palette knife. 13. Pencil to write on china or glass. 14. Agate etcher. 15. Kemper pen. 16. Pen to write on china or glass. (Courtesy K. B. Craft & Leather)

Alexander's Products

Brushes Sable is a loose term which could mean weasel hair which is cheaper or imitation sable hair, which is a blend of hair which looks like Kolinski Sable but is a much cheaper product.

Designer Paint Range A new range of onglaze paints for application to china. Due to advances in technology these paints are finely milled and do not exhibit grittiness in either appearance or physical nature. The high gloss and clear finish is chip resistant and the recommended firing temperature is 700–820°C. The success of these paints is due to three main factors:

1. bonding flux
2. glazing compounds
3. colouring agents.

Bonding flux is an additive which permits the basic components of the porcelain glaze and the ceramic onglaze paint to fuse together at a lower temperature to form a homogeneous bond. If too much is added, chipping can be a problem where the paint is applied heavily and colour deterioration can result. The flux Alexander's use in Designer Paints is a perfect combination for creating optimum paint adhesion, with no detrimental effects of colour loss or chipping.

Glazing compounds These are predominantly lead based compounds which readily dissolve other essential ingredients in glazes and in the paint pigments, to form a high, brilliant gloss appearance. These lead compounds have a lower melting point with a wide softening range which is what enables the paints to exhibit their outstanding characteristics.

Colouring agents The colouring agents are formulations of many chemicals, including cadmium, chromium, cobalt, copper, iron, manganese, nickel, tin, titanium and selenium, to mention the most common elements. The chemistry of forming colours is extremely complex and is further complicated by the reaction between the glaze and the chemicals used. For instance, cadmium based colours should not be mixed with other colours. The Designer Range has been extensively tested to ensure all colours will intermix, even pinks, reds and purples.

Lead content All ceramic onglaze colours, or china paints, require the addition of a large percentage of lead to enable them to work properly. This is the reason for the health warnings as required by the Australian Health Department on all the paint labels. It is important to follow general common sense when using powder paint. All paint dust should be kept to a minimum, hands should be washed and care should be taken not to transfer powders from hand to mouth.

Manufacture Most of the paints used in Australia today are manu-factured in Germany or England and there is a massive range available which seems endless when trying to select colours. Most colours are designed for commercial use (tiles, transfers, etc) with a wide range of firing temperatures, fast firing, slow firing, underglazes, and onglazes. The Designer Paint Range has been developed from the paints considered most suitable for painting by hand. The recommended firing temperature is 700–820°C.

Ferrule   There is a difference in the ferrules used in the production of brushes. Alexander's consider that nickel plated brass ferrules are the best and most suitable for the uses to which porcelain painters put their brushes. The various types of ferrules are listed in descending value:

1. Nickel plated brass *seamless*
2. Nickel plated *soldered*
3. Clear anodised aluminium seamless
4. Aluminium seamless (not anodised)
5. Soldered tin
6. Unsoldered tin.

A painter's hands would soon turn black using an aluminium seamless ferrule (not anodised). The term 'silver' may imply that it is a cheaper ferrule and not a nickel plated brass ferrule. Therefore the description of a brush which reads 'Sable hair silver ferrule' would suggest a cheaper brush using inexpensive (so called) 'sable' hair with a nickel plated soldered ferrule.

Flo-line brush   Full bodied Kolinski sable brush with a built in liner.

Golds   *Liquid Bright Gold AA grade*
Degussa 11% Liquid Bright Gold
Liquid Burnish Gold premium AA grade
Professional Liquid Burnish Gold 30%
Gold For Glass Low firing gold (520–630°C) especially for glass. Fires *bright gold* on top and underside of glass.

Golds and lustres   Simple rules which must be followed are:
Firing Allow gold or lustre to dry properly before firing. For best results, fire between 680–820°C. As ventilation is most important do not load kiln too closely and leave bungs out until approximately 500°C to allow gases and contaminants to escape. Always allow kiln to cool slowly with bungs in place.

Application Porcelain surface must be clean and dust free. Use a separate brush for each colour and keep clean. Use gold and lustre thinners to clean brushes. Gold and lustres should be applied in an even tan coloured coat, not too heavily and with only one coat per firing. Applied over bisque or matt surfaces a dull finish will be the result. May be applied by brush, stippled or sponged to achieve different effects. To slow drying time for large areas, a little thinner may be applied.

Storage Will last longer if stored in tightly sealed containers in a cool dark place. If gold or lustres thicken, add a little gold or lustre thinner at time of application.

Problems

Cracked or blistered gold—Applied too heavily or overfired.

Gold has areas of purple, blue or brown—Applied too lightly or over thinned.

Poor gold adhesion—Insufficient kiln ventilation. Applied over dirty glaze. Insufficient firing temperature.

White spots or spots of glaze showing through—Gold or lustres applied on a moist or dirty surface.

Dull or cloudy gold or lustre—Poor kiln ventilation. Contamination in gold or lustre. Dirty brush. Satin or matt surface.

Finger prints—Clean glaze before application and keep fingers clean of gold or lustre.

Odourless Brush Cleaner   Has a non irritating aromatic fragrance and is bottled in 500 ml containers. Has a similar solvent power to spirit of gum turpentine.

Oils and mediums   *Copaiba Medium Grinding Oil   Pen Oil   Rosemary Blend   Australian   Open   Medium   Grounding   Oil   Sabatella   Fat Oil   Clove Oil   Lavender Oil   Balsam of Copaiba*

Carey's Products

Carey's Base for Raised Gold or Enamel   Place a small quantity of powder on a glass mixing slab or tile and add a few drops of Carey's Enamel Medium. Grind until the mixture is crumbly. It is easier to have the mixture holding together well and then add a little more powder to bring it back to the crumbly texture required. Remember if it is too oily it will spread or crack when fired. Add perfectly clean turpentine until the mixture strings. If you add too much turpentine, keep mixing as the turpentine will evaporate. For easy application use the needle end of an *NT cutter*. Fire at 740°C, although it will take up to 800° without ill effect. (I find this an excellent dry powder paste which can be mixed with almost anything and which will withstand several firings. It may be left glossy white or coloured with ⅛ powder paint or the same proportion of mixed paint. It may be applied as is enamel or base for gold. It may be used as a fine or rough textured surface over a large area or as high build up, given sufficient drying time. It will tolerate additives such as pieces of glass, sand, stones etc, being painted or lustred and gilded. I have even replaced a large 2 centimetre chip from the rim of a plate with it by gradually building up the depression and edge in successive firings. *T.B.*)

Carey's Acid Etch Powder   Draw or trace design and apply Carey's Cover Coat over design and any other part not to be etched, eg the rim of a plate or a raised design on the porcelain. Mix a small amount of Acid Etch Powder with Carey's Seminar Medium, just thin enough to paint, and brush it over the exposed area. Pad with silk over cotton wool but do not over pad. Carefully remove Cover Coat. Fire to 760°C. If you wish to accentuate your design, such as roses, violets, forget-me-nots, leaves etc, apply Carey's Base for Raised Gold. Fire to 740°C. Before applying the Liquid Bright Gold, wash and rinse the china in clear water to rid it of any impurities. This is essential to prevent discolouration of gold. Be sure the china is completely dry before applying the gold. Fire to 720°C. A second application of gold should be given and again fired to 720°C. Apply gold a third time if necessary. For a different effect, apply the mixed powder with a piece of foam sponge. Instead of using Base for Raised Gold, the lines of the flowers may be penned with the Acid Etch Powder mixed a little thinner.

Carey's Copaiba Medium   Excellent quick drying medium.

Carey's Seminar Medium   Semi open, non sweating medium which is lint repellant and suitable for humid conditions. Open enough to allow for correction of work, while drying sufficiently to allow work to be fired. Do not use to mix and grind paints unless colour is to be used within a few days.

Carey's One Fire Medium   Ideal for painting in Dresden style. Paints must be mixed and applied smoothly. Fire to 800°C.

Carey's Grinding Oil   To mix powder paints, which will remain workable for seven or more years when kept in a covered container. Does not attract lint. Mixed colours are compatible with pen oils.

Carey's Pen Oil No. 2   A new and improved version of pen oil. May be added to mixed colours from palette and used and fired immediately.

Carey's Cover Coat   Waterbased masking agent which is not attacked by grounding oils.

Grounding Oil (Gwen's)   Slow drying oil with good colour absorption suitable for large areas.

Metallics and lustres   If you know you are going to apply metallics or lustres on a piece, apply one more coat of glaze to the piece than normal and fire as close to Cone 4 as possible. Clean piece with either Med-Mar Glaze Cleaner or acetone, remembering to wipe off the residue which is left by the acetone. Do not use rubbing alcohol to clean as it contains an oil.

Lustres may be applied by a variety of methods: a soft wide brush, an air brush or even your finger. Be sure your brush is clean and dry before using it to apply lustre. If using Mother of Pearl or Rainbow Opal, stroke the brush in different directions to increase the multi-coloured effect. Fire at 018 or 019 (standard cone). Allow the lustre to dry before firing, otherwise it will have a frosted appearance. If applied too heavily the lustre will chalk off after firing.

Gold, platinum and palladium   Follow the same basic instructions as for metallics and lustres. Apply the gold, platinum or palladium in a thin even coat and *do not* go over the unfired gold. If you do, these areas turn brown before firing and will be dull after firing. If the gold, platinum etc rubs off after firing it is because it was not fired high enough. Moisture will cause white spots after firing. Black specks are caused by dust or contamination before firing. If, when applying *Gold Bronze, Gun Metal* or *Red Copper*, it pools in deep recesses, it will fire off and leave bare areas showing. To rectify, clean with Glaze Cleaner and apply another coat all over. Do not touch up as this will show.

Hard spot If a large black spot appears and does not fire out it is caused when the slip is being poured. The glaze will be thin where the 'hard spot' is and lustres will turn black on this thinly glazed area. If there are tiny bubbles in the glazed surface or pin points in the ware, a blemish will result, particularly with lustres.

Frosting If Mother of Pearl appears dull there could be a number of causes. Too hot a fire or too long a firing cycle, poor circulation of heat, too heavy an application or firing before the lustre was dry.

Antique Etch   To give the appearance of erosion with age. Apply with an eye dropper or brush to cleaned greenware that will fire to Cone 06-05. Antique Etch is thin so the application must be controlled as it will immediately start to erode the greenware, causing interesting craters and raised areas. The amount applied governs the depth of erosion.

Antique Effect with Wild Dove   Iridescent grey brown lustre. Apply lustre to relief or textured work, rubbing back from raised areas. Repeat another complete coat and fire to Cone 019. On a plain surface first apply Antique Etch and when dry, fire and glaze. Coat with Wild Dove.

Blue Storm   Iridescent dark blue lustre. Use as Wild Dove or first apply Liquid Bright Gold or Liquid Bright Palladium or Platinum and fire. Then apply Blue Storm for a most unusual effect.

Metallic Flo-Base   Apply a heavy coat to a glazed and fired surface and immediately drop Liquid Bright Gold onto the wet areas so that it runs. Results in a lacy gold pattern.

Weeping Gold   (Not to be confused with Mottling Gold.) Apply over a glazed surface with as wide a brush as the object will permit. On a vertical surface, place loaded brush at the top and pull all the way down. A full brush will usually carry 25 centimetres. On a clear white glaze this will result in feathery runs of gold over a lavender pink background. Fire at Cone 019.

Weeping Platinum   As for Weeping Gold.

Painting on soap   Using Carey's Soap Medium and Carey's Soap Sealer. Mix china painting colours with a minimum of Soap Medium so as to leave them slightly dry on the palette. Moisten brush with Soap Medium and paint in the usual way. Do not use water with medium as drying time will be increased. Wipe outs are done with a brush moistened in the Soap Medium. Keep mixed paints in a covered container to prevent them from absorbing moisture from the air and wash brushes in water. When design is completely dry, thoroughly fill a ⅜ or ½ inch flat brush with soap sealer and flow it over the painted design without actually touching and scratching the design. Second and third coats may be applied when previous coats are completely dry, about 10 minutes. Full drying time is 24 hours. Wipe sealer from brushes and wash them in the special Sealer Brush Cleaner and dry. It is possible to use methylated spirits provided it is done immediately. If the Soap Sealer is contaminated with turpentine it will become milky.

Celia's Products

Celia's Petit Point   Used as a background and looks like tapestry. *Method*: Celia's Petit Point Mixture, small piece of sponge, fine wedding veil netting, 2 pegs.

Dry powder paints (not reds) can be added to the mixture for toning. Draw a pencil line around the area you wish to set off for the Petit Point base. Place a little of the mixture from the jar onto your palette and add turpentine to suit application. The mixture must be thin. It should run and spread on the palette. Dip the piece of sponge into the mixture and dab it onto the area to be treated. Take a large enough piece of net to pull round tightly underneath the article, twist and tighten then secure with the two pegs to hold the net tightly in place. Dip the sponge into the mix again and wipe evenly but not too thickly, over the area. Set aside to dry, eg for one hour under a lamp or beside a warm kiln, or overnight if dried naturally. When dry, remove the net and tidy the edges with a small pen-knife. Fire at 790–815°C. Left over mixture may be replaced in the jar. After firing, go over the Petit Point gently with a piece of wet and dry sandpaper to smooth. To paint, have your paints runnier and thinner than normal as the Petit Point base absorbs the paint like blotting paper. Reds will turn rusty brown.

Celia's Pre-mixed Acid Look   Meant to be used for fine designs using a mapping pen. Place a small portion from the jar onto the palette and mix with pure turpentine to a thin milky texture which flows smoothly from the pen or brush. Fire at 800°C and then apply lustres, Liquid Bright Gold or Silver, Burnishing Gold or Platinum and fire again at 800°C. The acid look should be applied very thinly as when painted with gold. The gold will turn black if the mixture is too thick.

Celia's Pre-mixed Glaze Acid   This mixture will remove the glaze where it is applied and the decoration can then be covered with lustres, gold or silver and have a matt finish. Mix well in the jar before use as the oil on top is part of the formula. Use masking lacquer to protect surface areas not to be treated and either sponge, paint or pen the mix onto your design. For pen or brush the mixture should be a little thicker than milk and slightly thicker for larger sponged areas. Just apply and do not smooth. Fire at 790°C. It is important to place the article where the temperature is correct, ie 790°C, in the kiln, as when the powder is rubbed off after firing the glaze will be unchanged if underfired, or the powder will be difficult to remove if it has been overfired.

Celia's Pre-mixed Gold Base Frost   To give a satin finish to gold painted china. Mix in the jar to the consistency of thick milk before use, as the oil on top is part of the formula. Use masking lacquer for areas not to be treated and cover two or three sponges with fine pure silk. Place some of the Gold Base mixture onto the palette and apply with a silk covered sponge. Use a second sponge to fine dab or buff so that you have a very fine application. Fire at 800°C. Apply Liquid Bright Gold in one or two coats, depending on the quality.

Celia's Pre-mixed Raised Paste or Coloured Enamel   Yellow pre-mixed raised paste is both for painting scrolls and trimmings which are to be covered with Liquid Burnishing Gold, Liquid Bright Gold or Platinum. For painting flowers, for example a blossom, use a No. 1, 2 or 3 pointed shader from Celia's French brush range. Take the mixture from the jar onto your palette, add a little pure turpentine, and stir with a palette knife until a very smooth texture and until there are no lumps of powder.

Method: Push paste to an edge around flower petal; then flatten the brush on the palette, no paste added, and pull down the strokes to the centre of the flower. This must be done quickly and neatly with no dry lumps to be seen—it does need a little practice. If any dry paste is left on the back of the brush, wipe away on a dry cloth. The mixture for painting flowers and leaves must be rather thin, just firm enough to hold the raised edge on the flower. Add pure turpentine frequently. For a pleasing embossed effect it does not have to be raised to extreme. Fire at 790–850°C. The raised paste and enamel can be used for scrolls, drops, large dots to small dots as a pattern. For scrolls, drops and dots use a mapping pen. When applying on the china as a drop, dip the mapping pen into the mixture then use the press, lift movement. The pre-mixed enamel and raised paste can be placed straight in the kiln; no drying time is needed when used as a painting material. If the enamel is used as a high texture application, then set to dry one or two days before firing. When gold or platinum is applied over raised paste and pre-mixed enamel, fire only at 600–650°C. *No more.*

White Raised Paste has a powder added to the mixture so that it can be used for scrolls, dots and lines on lustres, backgrounds and floral decorations, but where the pre-mixed enamel stands glossy and translucent, the raised paste will stand semi-matt. The white raised paste stands extremely white on dark backgrounds, very dark lustres, gold and platinum. It is very suitable for snow scenes. Fire at 790–815°C. If gold or platinum is used over white raised paste fire at no more than 650°. The raised paste may be stippled over a hairline or small crack.

Pre-mixed coloured enamels may be intermixed, with the exception of red and yellow. *Orange* matures at 700°C. *Salmon, Scarlet, Red, Deep Red* and *Black* mature at 740°C. *Rose Pink, Yellow, Light Green, Green, Aqua, Blue, Mauve, Brown* and *White* for mixing mature at 790–815°C. For a lighter tone add the pre-mixed coloured enamel to some pre-mixed white enamel. Do not add dry powder paint as this will disturb the formula and cause failure.

Degussa Products

Apparently Bright Gold was first developed in Meissen in 1830. The formula was kept a closely guarded secret for many years, and eventually came to the Degussa factory. There were initial problems with adhesion; however, after much experimentation a practical method was developed to produce large quantities of a good preparation at reasonable prices and comparatively easily, and during the last century the Degussa production has become world wide with subsidiary companies in many countries. Degussa expanded into a product range which included other precious metal preparations, and other decorating colour for glass, porcelain, enamel and earthenware; also stains, frits, glazes and special raw materials. The gold preparations have been developed to meet the many demands of commercial and amateur artists. They have to be compatible with various solvent systems and suitable for different application techniques. They must fire perfectly under extreme firing conditions, demonstrate chemical and mechanical resistance, and, as well, be in accordance with environmental and work regulations. Precious metal decorating products can be categorised according to:

1. Viscosity: liquid/pasty or solid (powder)
2. Fired appearance: glossy or matt
3. Precious metal content: gold, platinum, palladium or silver.

Liquid/pasty with a glossy finish are: Bright Gold, Bright Citron Gold, Bright Platinum, Bright Palladium, lustre.

Liquid/pasty with a matt finish are: Burnish Gold, Burnish Platinum, Burnish Palladium, Burnish Silver, Argalvan.

Solid preparations have a matt or satin finish and are: Painter's Gold, Powder Gold, Powder Platinum, Powder Palladium, and Powder Silver. The appearance of the bright preparations in their unfired condition is transparent, usually brown to black coloured liquids which look like varnish. They have a specific precious metal content.

Bright Gold is based on pure gold and fires with a red to yellow gold shade. The yellow Bright Golds contain a small percentage of silver.

Bright Platinum and *Bright Palladium* are based on platinum and palladium and have a grey/white metallic appearance when fired.

Lustres can be composed of precious metals as well as base metals which give them their metallic iridescent appearance.

Burnish and *Matt* preparations contain precious metal in fine powder or tinsel form. They are matt when fired and obtain a gloss by being burnished by sand, a glass brush or an agate pencil.

Painter's Gold is a chemically precipitated precious metal powder, frequently containing flux, which is mixed with thick oil for handpainted gold decoration. Also used for the dusting of steel prints and for the production of decals. Often contains mercury compounds and appropriate safety measures must be observed.

Dusting or *powder products* contain pure precious metal, mainly in flake form.

Bright Gold and *Bright Citron Gold* can be mixed with *Burnish Gold.* For a higher gold content, *Powder* or *Painter's Gold* may be mixed with Burnish Gold, however the flux content will vary and adhesion should be tested prior to application to piece.

The *gold content* and *Bright* preparations ranges between 6% and 24% and it is suggested that a 12% preparation be used for painting. For *stamping* no less than a 12% preparation should be used and a 15% is recommended. The *gold content* of *Burnish Gold* ranges between

12% and 40% and 16.5% is standard for liquid preparations, while paste has a content of 28%. A higher content is used for stamping, up to 30%. There are special preparations, eg *High Temperature, Fast Firing Gold* which generally has a higher gold content of up to 60%. The thickness of a layer of *Burnishing Gold* is three to six times that of *Bright* preparations and it is therefore more durable (and more valuable).

Storage   The maximum recommended storage time is approximately one year as the preparations are subject to changes during storage and become more viscous. This can be remedied by the addition of thinning oil. *Bright Citron Golds* may be stored from six months to one year after which they become so thick they are no longer applicable. *Black Burnish Golds* also become so thick in six months that it is difficult to use them. Other preparations become fluid during storage and should also be used within six months. If preparations are not to be used immediately they may be stored in the refrigerator or cool cellar. Precious metals are formulated for the various surfaces to which they are to be applied, such as porcelain, earthenware, majolica, glass and enamel. The object to be painted must first be thoroughly clean and free from dust, fingerprints, water stains and any other impurity. It is usually sufficient to rub with a textile or leather cloth which has been dampened with water and ethyl alcohol. However, if detergent must be used, a thorough rinsing is necessary as the detergent will leave a thin film on the surface. Glass to be fired may be treated with a 'mudding mixture', which mainly consists of ochre with the addition of copper sulphate to improve the adherence of Bright Gold; this creates a spotless fired film on the exterior surface and a more beautiful appearance on the interior surface. Other preparations are for frosting the glaze or glass by etching, or by firing a flux or colour. *Simili incrustation* is the decoration of edges with matt firing colours or gold base coats. The fired base colour is then painted with Bright Gold and fired again at a slightly lower temperature. The various methods of application include painting, edging, printing, spraying or machine transfer. *Bright Gold* should not be shaken as this may have an unfavourable influence or damage the decoration. *Burnish* preparations should be shaken very well prior to use and from time to time during the application. *Screen printing* preparations such as Burnish Gold pastes are intentionally more viscous and it is necessary to add thinning oil to attain the correct consistency prior to application.

Thinning oil needs to be used as there is loss of solvents through evaporation, however, this should not exceed 20% to 25% of the precious metal content. For *edging* and *spraying* a thin volatile oil is used, and painting a *large flat surface* requires a medium-flat oil and *stamping* a fat oil. There are a variety of oils available for the different requirements.

Environmentally-Friendly Burnish Gold preparations do not contain *mercury* and are more voluminous and therefore have to be applied in a thicker layer to attain the same gold content. They also contain a larger quantity of resin and appear more viscous and definitely require the correct thinning oil. Higher temperatures require a fatter oil. The more recent formulae should be applied with a smooth constant flow with no overlap, as these areas may be obvious and may also craze and crack.

Screen printing Decals are produced by means of a silk screen or it is possible to apply the design directly to the surface with the aid of a screen. There are screens available with the correct mesh to suit Bright preparations and Burnish preparations.

Offset printing generally uses high grade powder golds with a content of nearly 100% for the production of decals. The addition of a flux is necessary for adhesion.

Steel printing Painter's Gold is mixed with varnish or flux and printed onto tissue paper. However, it is also possible to use thickened Liquid Bright or Burnish Gold if the print on the tissue paper is transferred immediately to the piece for decoration. The addition of some varnish is most helpful. For indirect application, powdery precious metals are dusted onto the pre-printed gold surface and fired. As the basic surface already has a flux it is not necessary to use flux for this firing.

Stamping The application of gold by rubber stamp is generally thinner than when painted on and therefore requires a higher content gold preparation. This is poured onto a plate and treated with a rubber roll or spatula until the necessary consistency is obtained through the evaporation of the solvents, with consequent increase of the gold content. There are specially developed stamping oils available for this work and the addition of only a very small quantity is necessary.

Machine application is for the decoration of large quantities of ware with the same design. There are edging and stamping machines which apply the gold with both brushes and rollers.

Spraying Used to decorate large surfaces. After application the painted layers of the precious metal dry to a relatively hard surface and are relatively insensitive to dust. They may be handled with caution, taking care not to scratch or knock the object or deposit impurities on the surface.

Firing There are two separate phases in the firing of precious metals and lustres. First is the evaporation of fumes when the organic components are volatilised, carbonised and finally completely burned off with the oxygen in the air with increasing temperature. The precious metal layer starts to develop at the end of this phase when the temperature is approximately 420°C. It is essential that there be sufficient oxygen in the kiln during this phase and that the kiln be ventilated for this purpose and to allow the fumes to escape. In the firing of the preparation the flux additions and the metal oxides of the precious metal and lustre layers interact with the silicate components of the glaze, the glass or the enamel and cause mechanical adhesion through a temperature range of 520 to 830°C. If the kiln heats too quickly the time/temperature curve could cause a bright preparation to fire dull or matt or the development of the adhesive power could be reduced. The evaporating fumes could cause problems in the early firing stage and Bright Gold, particularly Bright Citron Gold, may fire dull. In extreme cases, insufficient ventilation could lead to the decomposition of a decoration, especially if the ware is closely stacked or loaded. Contours and shapes of borders may blur or even bleed during the firing process. If air vents cannot be left open, it is advisable to slightly open the door during the initial stages of firing, ie, up to approximately 420°C. The layer of precious metal which is produced during the firing process is very sensitive to fumes or other reducing gases; a lack of oxygen prevents the precious metal from fusing with the glaze, allowing it to be easily wiped off after firing. Bright preparations will lose their brilliance and metallic appearance without sufficient ventilation.

Temperatures used to fire the precious metal preparations allow for the time/temperature curve to be sufficient to cause the precious metal to fuse with the glaze, glass or enamel. The temperature recommended signifies the peak temperature in the muffle and the temperature of the hottest zone in a continuous kiln. In normal kilns heating is terminated when the required temperature is reached and additional 'soak' is usually not necessary. When firing glass the temperature should be maintained within distinct limits to avoid deformation of the glass and it may prove necessary to maintain the highest permissible temperature for approximately 10–30 minutes in order to obtain sufficient adhesion. The firing temperature has to vary according to the ceramic base materials and is dependent on the softening point of the glaze or glass. A guide for the conventional firing of porcelain is approximately 800°C, for glass approximately 500–580°C, and for enamel 700–800°C. Test fires should be performed on all surfaces to be painted as not all are suitable for decoration with precious metals. *Too high* a temperature will reduce the adherance of the precious metal layer and may cause an unattractive appearance or even the disappearance of the preparation. On soft glazes, colours or enamels the fired precious metal may crack (which may be desirable in some cases). On an ivory porcelain glaze, Bright Gold and Bright Platinum are very sensitive to excess heat and, with a temperature 30–40°C in excess, will adhere badly or not at all. The same excess in temperature will not adversely affect a normal layer of gold on white porcelain. Bright Citron Gold will lose its characteristic green colour and, according to the degree of excess heat, will become yellowish or reddish. Silver containing Burnish Golds will turn from green to yellow to red at excessive temperatures. The longer the firing cycle, the lower the temperature to obtain the same effect.

Too low a temperature will reduce the adherance of the precious metal to the surface.

Bright preparations need little attention once removed from the kiln. In some cases of certain glazes or glass the bright preparation may have a matt film which may be easily removed with a wet cloth. To check adhesion of decorated glass after firing, the ware should be dipped into water or wiped with a wet cloth; humidity could influence the adherence at a later date if it is not satisfactory at this stage. The bright decoration on glass may be overcoated with a ceramic flux and refired to refract the gloss of the gold and protect it against mechanical stress; this causes electrical isolation as well.

Burnish preparations have a dull, non-metallic appearance and have to be polished or burnished, either with moist fine sand or a glass brush. A spectacular finish will be obtained with the use of an agate or bloodstone or steel wool. This mechanical burnishing will effect the cohesion of the gold particles and improve the adherence. This procedure improves resistance to the chemical influence of detergents or acidic foods as well as enhancing durability, brilliance and attractiveness. The karat value of Bright Gold decoration can be designated at 22–24 karat and that of Bright Citron Gold approximately 17 karat. The karat value of Burnish Gold ranges between the two. The content of reddish golds is about 22 to 24 karat and of green Burnish Golds about 18 karat. Powder golds range in value from 19 to 24 karat. The thickness of the gold decoration also has to be taken into consideration.

Floral Products

Acid Under Base   A texture paste applied with a sponge, brush or pen to the porcelain surface and fired at 780–815°C. Gold or lustre may be applied over the matt area to give an etched look without the use of acid.

Floral Enamel   A raised and shiny enamel originally developed for scroll work and dots and to be used in conjunction with Liquid Bright Gold. It should be mixed to a stiff consistency and penned on. If it is too sloppy or fired too high, it will flatten; however, it may be used in a 'sloppy' state and applied with sponge or a spatula. Colour may be added to the enamels but beware of reds as they will fire out. Lustre may be sponged over the fired enamel and this will effect a colour change. Enamel for stiff work should be fired at 780°C and up to 860°C for flat work.

Flux   A powder product mixed with medium to a stiff consistency for the application of glass beads which are designed to stay on, or for a bed for *glass sand* to be sprinkled into and chipped off. Fire to 780–810°C for glass to fuse. Glass can be chipped off with a spatula but chip down and away from eyes. Gold and lustre can now be painted on this unglazed area for a matt effect.

Grounding Oil   Thick oil used for solid colour effect. Oil is spread evenly with a brush or sponge, adding turpentine if too thick and sticky. Pat off excess oil with a sponge covered with silk and apply dry powders evenly and not too thickly as they will chip off if too heavily applied. Do not open kiln door until cold.

Liquid Bright Gold   Will mature at 600°C. Paint over bare porcelain or enamel for a shiny effect or over Acid Under Base or paint for a matt appearance.

Lustre   Applied with pen, brush, sponged on or dipped in water. Several light coats are more effective than one or two heavy coats. Various colour combinations may be used, however it is advisable to use lighter colours first.

Masking Lacquer   Painted over a dry plate for an edge or design which is ground or lustred on; the masking lacquer is peeled off and the piece fired. Brushes are cleaned with methylated spirits or acetone. Cover Coat serves the same purposes as Masking Lacquer but is water based.

Metallic paints   Comprehensive range of colours available. May be grounded or multidusted with other compatible colours. May be used for normal painting or, thickly applied, they may be used to enhance ordinary paints. Fire 780–900°C.

Raised Paste   Yellow paste used for scroll work. Fire at 780–815°C and paint with Roman or Unfluxed Gold. May be used for stamens on flowers in dot form.

Texture Coat   A powder which may be used with a variety of liquids to achieve a stiff crackled appearance. Mix with milk, lemonade, glycerine, oil based mediums, etc, for different effects. Applied with pen, sponge or spatula. May also be mixed with tin and zinc oxides. Different kiln temperatures will give different effects (780–860°C). Colour may be added to the mixture or the fired product painted with golds or lustres.

Floral Fun with Texture

Requirements
Floral Flux
Floral Water Based Medium
Floral glass beads
Floral Texture Coat
Floral Liquid Bright Gold
Floral Liquid Bright Platinum
Floral lustres
Floral metallics

Sketch a design onto the porcelain. Mix flux with water based medium and paint design with mixture. Cover fluxed area with glass beads and fire to 815°C. Chip off glass bead layer and decorate with *gold, platinum, lustres, metallics* or *paint.* If powdered paints and metallics are mixed with water based medium they may be applied during the same firing.

Texture Coat may be used to add raised surfaces to your design. Mix with water based medium, apply to design, fire and decorate with *gold* or *platinum.*

Glass beads Mix flux with water based medium, add glass beads and apply the mixture with a palette knife to the porcelain. For an enamel-like appearance fire to 1000–1100°C before any colour is painted on. For a normal appearance, fire to 800°C.

Copper enamel may be added to some designs and best results are obtained if it is mixed with water based medium and applied on the last firing.

Fay Good's Products

Australian Open Medium   An open medium used for painting and mixing paints. If desired, paints may be mixed with this medium and painting done with copaiba medium. Paints will keep indefinitely if mixed with this open medium.

Citrus Solvent   Turpentine substitute and a boon for those allergic to turpentine.

Dresden Base for Raised Gold   Can be mixed with *any* medium you wish. Can be put on top of wet paint. Liquid Bright Gold can be fired on top of the scroll work done with this powder. Can be fired repeatedly. Fire to 016–017 (780–820°C).

Dresden Raised Enamel   Mix with enamel medium and pure gummed spirits of turpentine. Used for jewelling work. Very hard enamel. Can be coloured with powder paint if desiring to make coloured enamel. Fire to 016 or 017 (780-820°C). Can be fired many times if necessary.

Dresden Thinners　Used to thin raised paste after mixing with Dresden Raised Paste Medium. Also good for those allergic to turpentine. Can also be used for pen oil.

Enamel Medium　Mix enamel powder with a few drops of this medium until crumbly consistency, thin with pure gummed spirits of turpentine until it strings.

Essence of Grasse　(French Fat Oil) May be used to mix paints, to ground etc, but cannot be used as painting medium.

Essence of Chamarre　An open hyperallergenic medium used for mixing and painting. Paints will keep open indefinitely when mixed with this medium. If desired, copaiba medium may be used to paint.

French Acid Etch Paste　Used as a substitute for acid etching. Mix powder with any medium you would like. Apply only a thin wash of mixture in the design of your choice, ie scrolls, flowers etc. Fire to 016 (800-820°C). Second fire coat with Liquid Bright Gold and fire to 018 (760°C).

Grounding Oil　Cover area you wish to ground with this medium and then pad with very fine silk until only a thin, very even wash of oil is left. Cover with dry powder paint, remove excess and fire. This grounding oil will stay open longer than most and it is important to pad it well. You do not need to have a lot of oil on the china.

Ground Resist　Red plastic film painted on areas to protect from grounding, paint, golds etc. Water soluble. If too thick, add a drop of water and clean brushes in water. It is advisable to keep separate brushes for this resist.

Grounding Resist—Green　Acetone based film, stronger than red plastic film. Peels off easily before firing. For use in conjunction with air brushing or water based mediums. Clean brushes with acetone or nail polish remover.

Lead in paints　The reason for stating the firing temperature on the label of paint phials is that all paints contain a certain amount of lead, and the danger lies in the paints not being sufficiently matured in the firing and then being put to domestic use. Correct firing is essential so that the leachable lead content does not cause lead poisoning.

Medium for Raised Paste　Add a few drops to the raised paste powder until it is a crumbly consistency and then add pure gummed spirits of turpentine until stringy.

Metallic Colours for Grounding　Grind powder on a tile with completely denatured alcohol (methylated spirits) and allow to dry completely back to powder. Apply grounding oil to area to be grounded and pad very well. Place dry metallic colour onto oil and lightly rub into oil with a cotton ball. It is not necessary to use a mop brush as this powder flies more than normal powder. Fire to 016–017 (800–820°C). *All on-glaze colours fire at 800–840°C (017–016). All reds will take a high firing.*

Pen Oil Add a few drops to powder paint and mix to ink consistency. It may be mixed in larger quantities and stored in a glass jar.

Pre-mixed Enamel Stir in jar well. Remove a small amount onto a mixing tile. Add only pure gummed spirits of turpentine if necessary. Can be refired repeatedly. Fire to 016 or 017 (780–820°C).

Pre-mixed Raised Paste Take a small amount from the jar and add only pure gummed spirits of turpentine until stringy and creamy. Fire to 017. Do not take out of the kiln while hot. Allow the kiln to become completely cold before removing article. Coat with any of the golds.

Dresden Raised Paste and Gold Underlay Grind powder on a glass slab with completely denatured alcohol. Allow to dry back to powder. Mix powder with Essence of Grasse or Dresden medium (for raised paste) until like pie dough, then add only pure gummed spirits of turpentine or Dresden raised paste thinners until creamy. Fire to cone 017 (800°C). Do not take out of the kiln while hot. Allow the kiln to become completely cold before removing the article. This paste can be coated with Liquid Bright Gold, Roman, Unfluxed or Liquid Burnishing Golds. Fire again to 018 (760°C).

Note: Paste should not be applied too raised, only a light relief decoration.

Ruff-It Texture paste in form of white powder which may be mixed with most solutions, each of which gives a different result. Fired at a range of temperatures which will also have an affect on the appearance of the fired paste.

Kitty Drok Products (*Courtesy of Alexander's*)

Covercoat Water soluble red liquid which dries to form a plastic film to cover and mask previously painted areas when grounding or using lustres or gold etc.

Copaiba Medium Open painting medium but not as open as the *Odourless Medium.*

Crystal Clear Glaze Gives a high gloss to painted areas. *Do not* apply over red. Fire at 780°C.

Grounding Oil Thick quick drying oil which does not attract dust. Powder paints may be applied straight away. For large areas, add a drop or two of turpentine to keep it open.

Mixing Medium Stays open indefinitely but does not allow paint to spread. Does not attract dust and may be used as pen oil if mixed with paint from the palette and thinned with turpentine. To preserve brushes: wash in turpentine and wipe off excess. Dip into mixing medium to keep brush hairs supple and soft.

Odourless Medium   A medium which does not have a strong smell and has more grip for paint on the porcelain surface. A very open medium which dries sufficiently to be non-slippery and for use for dry dusting.

Premixed Enamels   Ten colours available and it is possible to apply gold over the enamels.

Petit Point   Apply over a glazed surface to obtain a bisque finish. May be used to obtain a raised effect under gold work as well as in place of Acid Under Base. May also be used for repair work, repairing chips or flaws. Dries quickly to allow easy removal of netting. *Do not* apply *red* over Petit Point paste.

Josephine Robinson Glass and Porcelain Products

Etched Look   A white powder compound which, when applied to glass and fired, gives the appearance of etched glass. There is also a *Matt Etched Look.*

Glass Crystals   Clear and coloured glass crystals suitable for decoration on glass, such as patterns, borders and texture on glass surfaces. To use, paint glass glue all over the desired area and sprinkle the glass crystals liberally over. Clean glass and fire in the range of 540–580°C.

Glass Metallic Paints   Metallic paints suitable for the low glass firings. Mix with Josephine *Water Based Medium.*

Glass Pearl Range   Pearlised colours developed for painting on glass. Interesting effects are created when colours are applied over dark backgrounds, especially blue or black. Fire at 560–600°C.

Peelable Resist   A resist for use on both glass and porcelain.

Pollyanna 'New' Enamelling Plus   An enamel for porcelain which can be fired more than once at 800°C. May be coloured with dry or premixed paint and painted over wet paint for highlights. It is suitable for scroll work and the application of gold, paint and lustre once it is fired. It may also be used as *'flow' enamel* with the addition of turpentine. There is no drying time and it will not pop off.

Pollyanna 'New' One Fire Wet Grounding   Mix dry paint with *Pollyanna Grounding Oil* until crumbly. Add lavender oil until the consistency of pen oil and apply with *sponge brush* by dipping 'brush' into the mixture and pouncing onto china. Keep pouncing until you hear a smacking sound. Fire at 800°C (some pinks a little higher). *Clean sponge brush* in Preen or similar product and rinse in cool water. Dry on paper towel.

Portrait Paints   Powder paints specifically developed in flesh tones for painting portraits.

Silk Look   A new white powder product for glass decoration. May be painted on or grounded with *Pollyanna Grounding Oil.* Fired at 520–580°C. The higher it is fired the more transparent it will become.

Sponge brush   Soft fine sponge with wooden handle. An invaluable tool with many uses. May be washed after use.

Margaret Butter

New Petit Point Gloss Enamel   A gloss Petit Point which dries in 30 minutes, is fired at 800°C and may be painted. It is kind to brushes. Add only pure turpentine to suit application.

New White Gloss Enamel   Does not require a drying time. Add only pure turpentine to suit application.

Hints

Students

1. Arrive on time. However, if you do arrive late, try not to disrupt the class. They have paid for their lesson. Do not stay later to make up time as your teacher has planned her day.

2. Paint the class projects. There is time at home for you to do anything which is not included in your teacher's curriculum. Also, if you do not want to do what the class is doing this week, it will not be long before you do want to and your teacher is going to be exasperated at having to say it all again!

3. Take care of borrowed aids and designs.

4. Have all your own equipment labelled.

Things to do before painting a piece

1. Remove labels, tags etc.

2. Clean with methylated spirits.

3. Check which way is up by looking for hanging holes. Mark top with graphite or grease pencil.

4. If flawed, plan your design to disguise flaw.

5. Plan the line of your design and, if you must, draw a pencil line to keep you on it. Draw another shorter design line across it so that you know where to branch your groupings.

6. Sketch some of the blossoms you intend to paint on paper, cut out and position them on the plate until you are pleased with the composition. *Do not* pick up the brush, paint a flower, turn the plate around three times and paint another at random at half or twice the size of the first one and hope to join the two together. It only works for the experienced.

7. Think in threes. Three of everything, light, shade, values, colour (that is three colours on the one petal or leaf, not the whole design). Large, medium, small areas; original colour, shaded colour and reflected colour. Foreground, middle distance and background. *Threes!*

8. Leave plenty of light. Even dark areas have light.

9. Paint a different colour over a fired colour for a translucent effect—one of the advantages of painting on porcelain.

10. Keep your palette clean and dust free but do not be discouraged by a messy palette, it simply means that you are mixing the loads on your brush and blending your colours, for which you are to be congratulated. Just clean up after each painting session.

11. When painting a flower always start with the centre, even if you will not be able to see it in the finished painting. The centre is the part which holds the flower together and, therefore, the most important part. It has to be there. If you paint the petals to the centre, the sepals to the centre and the stem to the centre, your flower will be in proportion.

Things to do after painting a piece

1. Check for design faults.
2. Clean edges.
3. Clean base or underside.
4. Sign it.
5. Turn upside down or cover with gladwrap.

Too much oil can cause paint to run in the kiln. Some open mediums should be used *very sparingly*. If your painting *looks* wet then it is probably too wet.

Hold your plate in the palm of your hand. *Thumbs leave prints!*

Put *cotton wool* pad soaked in turpentine or oil of cloves in your palette if your paints are not mixed with an open medium or grinding oil. Hopefully, it will keep them fresh a little longer.

Mix *grainy powder paints* with methylated spirits or turpentine prior to mixing with normal grinding oil.

Do not put nylon net in your turpentine jar. It will shred your brushes.

Add *flux* to a last minute touch of colour if you want to fire it at a lower temperature than normal because of pastes or enamels in the kiln.

When painting *medallions* and smaller pieces of porcelain, sit them on a piece of plasticine or Bluetack onto a slightly larger shard or tile to facilitate holding them. They may be transported to the kiln and fired, still in the same manner.

Place your *vial of gold* on a piece of plasticine or putty and then in a slightly larger jar to stabilise it. If it spills, you will be faced with an expensive accident.

When painting *animals* or *portraits*, trace the subject onto clear *plastic*, outlinging all the features and colour changes in detail. Use this tracing to check your own work for shape and form by holding the pattern above your work.

Underfired pieces may be refired.

Most china colours will take a wide range of temperatures.

Paints, golds, lustres and glass to be 'slumped' may be fired in the same kiln load.

Dust and moisture will leave white spots on gold and lustres.

Homemade resist   Crush a light coloured piece of blackboard chalk to a fine powder and add some clear glue to make a thin paste. Add sufficient water to attain poster paint consistency. Apply. Dry thoroughly and fire with vented kiln. Brushes can be washed in water.

For a *bronze effect*, paint Roman Gold thinly over Russian Green.

A drop of Liquid Bright Gold into Opal or Mother of Pearl lustres will enhance the colours. Too much Liquid Bright Gold will turn the lustres grey.

Paint designs on real eggshells which have been blown. Gently and carefully pierce the top and bottom of the raw egg with a sharp needle. Blow through one hole and the contents will come out at the other end. Once the shell is empty (you can use the contents) and dry, paint it with your normal paints. Allow to dry. Spray with artists' finishing varnish. *Do not fire.* Or—decorate with Ceramic à Froid.

Do not wash porcelain blanks immediately prior to painting them as the porcelain may retain some of the moisture. This may affect your paints and the firing process.

Grounding   Mix a little dry powder in your grounding oil before application to enable you to see where you have covered the surface.

If you are masking an area of design prior to grounding first trace the design so that you will be able to find the masking lacquer easily after the powder has been applied.

Use masking tape for a straight line, particularly when dry dusting.

For a full rich colour, apply the powder as soon as the oil is sufficiently dry; for a lighter coating, wait until the oil is much drier as it will not absorb so much of the powder.

Do not *ground* where there is a freshly painted, unfired area nearby. The paint flies about and may adhere to the wet paint.

Firing   Do not place large flat tiles on the floor of the kiln or against the walls and elements as the heat distribution is uneven and may cause fractures.

Do not place wet pieces in the kiln as moisture may cause dullness.

Do not allow glazed surfaces to touch. They may fuse with one another.

Do not overcrowd; however a full kiln will give better results than one with just one or two pieces in it.

Do allow space between walls and pieces for expansion.

Do heat to dry out an infrequently used kiln before firing.

Do leave the air vents open until oils burn off and fumes escape.

Do place a saucer of vinegar on top of the kiln if you are concerned by the fumes during firing.

Do fire and cool slowly to avoid breakages.

Do place small medallions etc on Bluetack to fire so that they can be easily placed in the kiln.

If your *raised paste* will not string or lengthen easily, add a drop of enamel medium to it.

There will *always* be some *additional expenses.*

To choose a *design* for your porcelain blank, sketch the shape and *doodle* whenever you have a minute, are on the telephone, or waiting for someone. Doodling is often the answer to a difficult problem.

Try *doodling* to music and then searching your results for a design. A window or frame cut to the shape of your blank is helpful.

Matt silver will tarnish. It will need to be polished.

Paint porcelain *bisque* with paints mixed with *glycerine* if you do not have any lavender oil.

To protect *fine slender brushes* keep them in a coloured drinking straw.

To protect *pen nibs* keep them in a drinking straw.

Store your *grounding brush, blender or mop brush* with a tiny plastic bag over the hairs to keep out the dust. Inflate the bag and secure with an elastic band to prevent weight on the bristles.

Blend your *signature* with your painting. It should be obvious (who knows, it may be worth something), but not obtrusive, penned in a suitable colour and legible.

Do not *eat* while working or you may drop crumbs, salt or sugar on your work. These will all leave white spots in the fired paint, the reason being that the majority of foodstuffs are water based and fall onto the oil. The two do not mix!

Dull red, painted very very lightly, will produce a beautiful *pink.*

Use *disposable surgical gloves* (readily available from pharmacies) for finger wipe outs, if you are at all allergic, cleaning your palette, applying lustre with foam etc.

Vacuum out your kiln periodically to remove kiln dust. You will find your work much smoother and it will not require so much sanding.

Add *yellow* to *rose pink* to prevent it turning blue with firing.

Try not to fire a piece immediately after it has been painted. Look at it closely the next day to check for *faults*. It is said that these may be seen more readily in a *mirror*. View from all angles. Something which leaps out at you trying to attract your attention may be trying to tell you something!

All surfaces should be thoroughly cleaned before applying *gold*. Do not apply *gold* to painted but as yet unfired porcelain.

Allow *turpentine* to settle and the sediment to fall to the bottom and pour off the clean turpentine into another jar.

Flat tiles or *jewellery pieces* are easily raised with a palette knife so that fingers may be slid underneath to lift and carry, rather than on top where they leave prints.

Raised paste for gold is yellow. *Raised base* for gold is white.

Obtain an *antique look* by painting green lustre over fired gold.

Always paint a design inside a box for interest. Preferably on the inside of the lid as well as the base which would be covered by the contents.

Skies should be darker near the horizon.

Horizons should never cut the tile or blank in half.

Aim to use natural lines for your *line of design*. Contour lines in a landscape, fracture lines in stone or the character lines on the palms of your hands, and dare I say it— face?

A well designed tile or plate with your *name, address* and *telephone number* is good to have nearby when demonstrating. Viewers can take down particulars without interrupting to ask for a card.

A *highlight* left as you paint is always interesting. One wiped out later may not be.

When painting *trees and bushes*, stipple the tops with a *deerfoot stippler* for a muted, diffused effect.

Place your *eraser pencil* in the refrigerator and it will be easier to sharpen.

To *transport a kiln* line it with cardboard and pack the interior with pillows. Secure the lid or door and pyrometer and tie in place.

To *replace elements* which have popped out of their groove, heat the kiln for a few seconds, until the element wire is pliable, turn off the kiln and gently lengthen the wire by pulling open the coils slightly and replace them in their grooves.

When firing *glass lamps*, allow plenty of space between the walls (and elements) of the kiln and the lamp to prevent sagging.

Designs and monograms on cups are traditionally placed to the left of the handle.

Add a drop of fat oil (evaporate some turpentine in a shallow dish for several weeks and keep a small amount in a jar) to *blues and carmines* when painting a wash or tint. Too much fat oil will cause the paint to blister, but a little will help both the colour and adhesion.

Mother of Pearl may be used over fired paint.

Rose leaves are not spread out like a handful of playing cards.

Leaves should match the flower you are painting. Rose leaves do not really suit a daisy and vice versa.

For *deep, rich colours*, try lightly grounding and then painting over the top of the fired grounding.

If the darkest value in your design is next to the lightest value, the viewer's eye will go directly to that area.

Try silk screen printing a repetitive design on tiles.

When setting up an *exhibition* remember *quality* is more important than *quantity*.

A *concertina folder* is ideal for carrying a number of plates to class and to kiln.

Do not fiddle with *happy accidents*. Leave them alone!

Contemporary fruit: Squared and angled outlines make an interesting painting.

Hide defects and *flaws* on the porcelain surface with the darkest part of the design, a line, glass incising, texture, etc.

Did you know that Renoir (yes, the real one!) painted on porcelain before he painted in oils?

Use *methylated spirits* to clean your work after *grounding and dusting*. It will not run into the applied powder paint as turpentine does.

Plates covered with Gladwrap may be carried face to face without slipping.

Forgotten a box for your freshly painted plate? Tape it face down to your palette or to a hard plastic covered book. You do cover your expensive reference books with plastic don't you?

Look at your painting in sections through a frame. You may be surprised.

Thin *lustre resist* with water.

When painting a group of flowers have each of them facing in slightly different directions.

Do not dry *raised paste* artificially.

Do not use *Liquid Bright Gold* over *raised paste* as it will turn black.

Do not use *glazes* such as *Crystal Clear* over iron colours (reds, red browns and some of the less expensive pinks) as they will disappear.

For those who cannot paint roses. Lightly sketch a rose design in *very* fine line penwork, using Violet of Iron for your outlines. Have three roses, supporting leaves and stems and a few faintly outlined shadow leaves and shapes. If you have used pen oil, fire; if you have used simple syrup, Coca-cola or something similar, once it is dry, you may immediately rouge in a creamy yellow rose, using the pad of your finger dipped in oil and then, in yellow paints, adding deeper colour at the base of the bowl of the rose with an old gold and a little Golden Brown. Use the Golden Brown to give a rich centre colour and depth. Stay within your outlines and mould the contours of your leaves and petals with slightly deeper colour towards the outer edges. Keep only a light application in the centres. While you have the yellow tones on your finger, paint a few highlights on the leaf areas. Now paint in a pale pink rose using Blood Red very lightly for the outer petals and a little more heavily for the shading. There is such a wide range of values in Blood Red you may not have to use another colour for variation. Add a little reflected colour to your leaves with the pink. Paint in the third rose with a slightly darker tone of red or orange and paint in your leaves in the same manner using greens and blues. You may have to use a cotton bud for the fine stems. Clean the colour off the white porcelain outside the lines and fire. A simple *one fire finger painted plate* that the rawest newcomer could produce as a morale booster.

When choosing your porcelain blank take into consideration the basic principles of composition, the natural surroundings of your subject and your treatment of it.

Know your subject. Use fresh flowers when possible and try to draw outlines, various aspects, the leaves, buds, etc.

Apply a line of dots along a marked ruler for even spacing and accuracy. Use the curved edge of a plate or saucer, marked with a plate divider, for a circle or arc.

Try to salvage *hardened lustre* with lavender oil. You will probably not have a true colour, however the gloss is usually there.

Clouds are not all white! Not all clouds are white!

Before firing *gold* applied to *raised paste* (fired of course), clean up the edges with a craft knife once the gold has dried.

Paint with *pink* or *rose very lightly* in the first fire. It can be disastrous if applied with a heavy hand.

Paint *yellow roses* a very pale grey to form and mould the shape and follow with washes of colour in subsequent firings.

A mixed load of lustre and painted objects in the kiln will improve the gloss of the glaze.

Pinks and rubies will appear yellow or brown if underfired and blue toned if overfired.

The *sharpest detail* is found in the *middle values*, not in the highlighted areas or the darker shadow areas.

Matt paints will be glossy if fired high.

For shadow filled backgrounds, wash a different colour over a fired background and wipe out shapes. Fire and repeat with another colour wash. Fire again. Do not overdo it.

Make *highlights* larger than required for the first painting. They seem to get smaller whether you plan it or not.

Rocks, when painted, should look well settled into the ground and not about to topple over.

Texture is both *visual* and *tactile.*.

Do clean your palette, preferably after each painting session and certainly before every lesson and seminar.

Do listen to the instructor.

Do ask questions and *listen* to the answers.

Do show the *baby photos* before or after the lesson, not during it.

Do remember that a seminar is where you go to be shown a new technique. Then, go home and perfect it.

Do take a notebook and *use it.*

Do cover a study with clear plastic, especially if it is not yours!

When painting wildlife pay attention to eyes, claws and facial features etc.

Very fine broken outlines of enamel in one or two areas of your design will help with strength and contrast.

Link your design with scrolls, lattices and grounding.

An edge of gold may be all your plate needs to really 'finish' it. And a band of gold frequently enhances an otherwise plain vase.

Insect eaten leaves make a more realistic and interesting painting.

If you do not like your finished product, lightly ground or dust it, outline the design which shows through in black, gold or enamel and paint in a background.

Use a photocopier to enlarge or diminish designs, or have colour photos reproduced in larger sizes for studies for seminars.

Suppliers

New South Wales

The Porcelain Palette
(Sandra Brown)
Rear 23 Beaufort St, Northmead
2150
(02) 6308025

Pots Plus
45 Restwell St, Bankstown 2200
(02) 7900449

Porcelain Arts Centre
14 Moore Ave, West Lindfield 2070
(02) 466428

Porcelain Art Videos
PO Box 331, Northbridge 2063
(02) 9581724

Wendy's Wool N' Things
3 Littleton St, Riverwood 2210
(02) 5342491

The Junction Gallery
17 Kenrick St, The Junction,
Newcastle 2290
(049) 695040

Margaret Butter
32 Ellis St, Dundas 2117
(02) 6303200

Kedumba Studio & Gallery
(Marion Goard)
5/124 Rowe St, Eastwood 2122
(02) 8585104

Jaybee's China Supplies
'Aquila', Grenfell 2810
(063) 431616

Vincent's Porcelain Supplies
87 Tamworth St, Dubbo 2830
(068) 027099 AH 821503

Russell Cowan
12 Leeds St, Rhodes 2138
(02) 7362033

Wagga Porcelain Supplies
(Dorothy Prest)
16 Amsterdam Cres, Wagga Wagga
2650
(069) 223785

Mona Vale Pottery Supplies
Bungan Court, Mona Vale 2130
(02) 9972112

Creative Craft
65 Magellen St, Lismore 2480

Jean Hill Studio
'Tomintoul', Windward Way, Milton
2538
(044) 551077

Porcelain Art Importers
Unit 2, Lot 3, Tucks Rd, Seven Hills
2147
(02) 6244955 AH 6266389

Queensland

Pottery Supplies Ltd
51 Castlemaine St, Milton 4064

Glen Baum Porcelain Art Studio
15 McIlwraith St, Auchenflower
4066
(07) 8701930

Nerang Craft Cottage
Lavelle St, Nerang 4211
(075) 961991

Stafford Craft
Minimine St, Stafford 4053

Iris Hopkins
27 Kedron St, Wooloowin 4030
(07) 2623407

Dania Studio
59 Cupania St, Mudjimbe Beach
4564

Panaroo Porcelain
17 Hamilton St, Nowra 4718

Elizabeth Dunn
109 Witt Ave, Carrara 4211
(075) 583269

Western Australia

Jackson's Ceramic Craft
391 Hay St, Subiaco 6008

The China Cellar
164 Brighton Rd, Scarborough 6019

Porcelain Art Supplies
128A Canning Hwy, South Perth
6151

Mayama
16 McDonald St, Osborne Park 6017

Victoria

Patricia's Porcelain
(Patsy Meldrum)
16 Pinnacle Cres, Bulleen 3105
(03) 8509813

Bette's Porcelain Shoppe
558 Glenferrie Rd, Hawthorn 3122
(03) 8192992

D's China Painting Supplies
16 Mitchell St, Mentone 3194
(03) 5835011

Kelly's Porcelain Supplies
46 Acheron Ave, Mount Eliza 3930
(03) 7871188

M & J China
33 View St, Bendigo 3550
(054) 430336

Tiffany's
284 Union Rd, Moonee Ponds 3039
(03) 3700770

Diamond Ceramics
50 Geddes St, Frankston 3199
(03) 5604466

Grampian China Art
157 Main St, Stawell 3380
(053) 583488

Porcelain Pieces
17 The Boulevard, Heathmont 3135
(03) 7299133

The Painted Plate
101 Station St, Ferntree Gully 3156

Ocean Grove China
72E The Terrace, Ocean Grove 3226

Tasmania

Devon Art & Craft
154B Williams St, Devonport 7310

J. Walch
130 Macquarie St, Hobart 7000

Porcelain Arts
(Hazel M. Shepherd)
214 Main Rd, Gravelly Beach 7251
(003) 944777

Australian Capital Territory

K. B. Craft & Leather Supplies
(Kim and Bob Denning)
62 Oatley Court, Belconnen 2617
(062) 516918 AH 586158

A Peace of Porcelain
Ginninderra Village, Ginninderra
2617
(062) 302695

South Australia

Carey's
153 Payneham Rd, St Peters 5069
(08) 421304

Alexander's
6 Surrey Rd, Keswick 5035
(08) 2977055

Hanna's China Ware
64 Radford Rd, Anguston 5353
(085) 642630

The Gilberton Gallery
(Josephine Robinson)
101 Walkerville Tce, Walkerville
5081
(08) 3441688
5081
(08) 3441688

Fay Good
43 Devonshire St, Walkerville 5081

Arts and Parts
63A The Broadway, Glenelg South
5054
(08) 2941050

Crinklewood Gallery
79 Waterhouse Rd, Plympton 5038

The Brushstroke
448 Goodwood Rd, Cumberland
Park 5041
(08) 2712553

Warwick Art Centre
1166 South Rd, Clovelly Park 5042
(08) 2772968.

New Zealand

Strawberry Hill
PO Box 965, Newmarket, Auckland
(09) 796086

Calvin Trading Co Ltd
Box 165, Otaki
(069) 47486

Judith Gainsford
20 Melville St, Christchurch
(03) 598304

Pam Hobbs
23 Mulberry Place, Christchurch
(03) 525458

Cobcraft
24 Essex Street, (PO Box 32024),
Christchurch
(03) 667229

Shand China Company
19 Bristow St, Wanganui
(064) 50568

Sheryl Young
340 Kohimarama Rd, Auckland 5
(09) 582769

Individual Art Studio & Gallery
(Vivienne Bashford)
142 Somerfield St, Christchurch 2
(03) 321643

Affiliated Industries
152 Greenlane Rd, (Box 17-19
Greenlane), Auckland
(09) 542386

Potters Western Suppliers
Northway St, Te Rape, (PO Box
10-362, Hamilton)
497473

Coronet Gift Shoppe
395 Grey St, Hamilton
66440